Visual Basic Developer's Guide to UML and Design Patterns

Visual Basic® Developer's Guide to UML and Design Patterns

Yair Alan Griver
Matthew Arnheiter
Michael Gellis

SYBEX®

San Francisco • Paris • Düsseldorf • Soest • London

Associate Publisher: Richard Mills
Contracts and Licensing Manager: Kristine O'Callaghan
Acquisitions Editor: Denise Santoro-Lincoln
Developmental Editor: Benjamin Tomkins
Editor: Jill Schlessinger
Production Editor: Elizabeth Campbell
Technical Editors: Michael Sakhatsky and Steven Black
Book Designer: Kris Warrenburg
Graphic Illustrator: Tony Jonick
Electronic Publishing Specialist: Nila Nichols
Proofreaders: Elizabeth Campbell, Jennifer Campbell, Nathan Whiteside, Laurie O'Connell, Dave Nash
Indexer: Lynnzee Elze
Cover Designer: Design Site
Cover Illustrator: Jack D. Myers

Yair Alan Griver would like to dedicate this book, as he did with all the others, to his wife, Jan.

Matthew Arnheiter would like to dedicate this book to his family for their support and understanding through the years.

Michael Gellis would like to dedicate this book to his wife, Nechama, and children, Sori, Malky, Rivky, and Yosef Meir, who don't understand the significance of design patterns but still gave up some family time towards the book.

Finally, we'd all like to dedicate this book as well to the Gang of Four, whose book started us out on this path—and made our applications more maintainable and understandable.

FOREWORD

Design patterns, as applied to application development, provide ways to describe common solutions to common problems. This book is an excellent resource for learning about design patterns, how to describe them using UML, and how they relate not only to Microsoft Visual Basic, but also to application development in general. As you'll read in this book, you'll find that using design patterns can make you and your colleagues more productive.

Microsoft Visual Basic has had a long history of making developers productive in writing applications for Windows. Visual Basic 1.0 gave developers of all skill levels an easy, productive way to write applications for Windows. The next two versions added support for other technologies such as multimedia and e-mail, as well as integrating database access. When we shipped Visual Basic 4.0, we really moved into a much broader developer market. That version was the first time that VB had an enterprise edition that was specifically targeted at developers creating business applications. In subsequent versions we've added even more features that have enabled developers to easily create large distributed applications.

When Visual Basic started moving into this application space, the groups of developers at large companies became more diverse, adding Visual Basic programmers to the ranks that often consisted of people with skills in C and C++. As other tools and languages have become increasingly popular, the diversity in these groups has also increased. This trend presents new challenges for Visual Basic developers, as they interact and work with developers and architects accustomed to using other tools and languages. Interacting with this wider audience sometimes can be difficult because these other tools and environments use different terminology, and therefore, so do the people who use those tools. As a result, communication between these developers and architects becomes more difficult.

Using common design patterns to describe a problem and solution, and using UML to visualize these patterns, provide a *lingua franca* for all developers. This common language increases productivity and reduces mistakes and misunderstandings. As a result of UML, these diverse groups can now easily communicate ideas, problems, and solutions without having to spend time educating each other about the intricacies and differences in their tools and languages.

I first met Alan and other developers from Flash Creative Management when I was a program manager on the Visual FoxPro team. Alan was a leader in the developer community and was often called upon to help us understand customers' needs, work out design issues, and work on goals, objectives, and feature definitions for the future versions of the product. He was always able to provide insight into the problems facing developers and how best to solve them.

When I moved into the Visual Basic group, I continued to work with Alan on similar issues. Since both of us have a background in FoxPro development, we were able to draw on our experiences using that product to help us discuss the problems facing developers, where the market was headed, and many other development-related issues. In a way, although I didn't know it at the time, we were using a rudimentary form of patterns.

We both had similar development experiences and knowledge of a given tool that helped us communicate. I remember several times that we'd have a problem getting each other to understand some feature or functionality and how it might be applied to Visual Basic. In these cases, we'd both compare our point to something we were familiar with in FoxPro, which invariably would get the other to see the point. Looking back, it's pretty clear that if we'd been using some of the design patterns described in this book, we'd have been even more effective at communicating.

Microsoft Visual Basic is a very powerful development environment, enabling a wide range of developers to create a broad spectrum of applications. Using the tools and techniques that you learn in this book, you will be able to better communicate your ideas and more easily understand your colleagues. In addition, you'll be able to make better design decisions as well as architect reusability and flexibility into your applications. The concepts provided in *The Visual Basic Developer's Guide to UML and Design Patterns* are very powerful and will enable you to increase your skills as a solution developer using Visual Basic.

Rob Copeland
Product Unit Manager, Visual Basic
Microsoft Corporation

ACKNOWLEDGMENTS

There are *tons* of people to thank in this book, as there has been for all the other books that we have written over the years. We're pretty sure that we'll forget some people, so please consider yourselves mentioned.

Our coworkers at Flash Creative Management: David Blumenthal, Ed and Elise Ziv, Lior Hod, Kamal Patel, Jayesh Patel, Joe Lax, David Sheer, Rick Hodder, Drew Georgopoulos, Nikolai Paradizov, Tony Stewart, Bryan Caplovitz, CT Blankenship, Jenny Brown, Beth Massi, David Kinne, Eric Zimmerman, Pablo Geralnik, Hector Geralnik. This book is theirs also. They all contributed ideas, code, text, and a fun place to return to when writing this book got to be too much. They also were able to take over for us on projects as deadlines neared. Thanks a lot fellow Flashers.

We would also like to thank the ton of folks who have been interested in patterns over the years and who have provided us with a lot of feedback during discussions at various developer's conferences and the Tech Ed or two at which we've spoken.

Kudos to our two tech editors, Steve Black and Michael Sakhatsky.

We'd like to offer a special thanks to the gang at Sybex who worked so hard in putting together this book: Jill Schlessinger, Ben Tomkins, Denise Santoro-Lincoln, Kristine O'Callaghan, and Melanie Spiller—who started our relationship with Sybex. Thanks guys…

To our parents and relatives who understood when we couldn't always get together so that we could work on this book.

And, to separate things out…

Yag would like to specially mention his cat, Chushie, who now has the dubious distinction of having been mentioned by three different authors in at least six different books ranging the gamut from Visual Basic, Visual FoxPro, SQL Server, and Design Patterns; and his dog, Kasey, who is truly a wonder dog.

Michael would like to specially mention his dear father and mother for their support in all his endeavors, and his brother Akiva because he likes to be mentioned.

Matthew would like to specially mention his parents for their understanding through the years and for giving him his first computer, a TRS80, model 1.

CONTENTS AT A GLANCE

CONTENTS

INTRODUCTION

Welcome to our latest book. This introduction will discuss the purpose of this book and the various sections into which it has been divided. Designing an application is a complex task and, over time, as applications have become more complex, certain standards for analyzing business problems and designing the software solutions to fix them have come to the forefront. This book covers two of those standards, design patterns and the Unified Modeling Language (UML) diagrams used to document them.

Who Should Read This Book?

This book is geared towards intermediate to advanced Visual Basic (VB) developers, especially those who have a pre-existing interest in design patterns, but haven't been able to understand the samples that have typically been shown in C++ or Java. Our goal is that this book will allow you to understand the patterns that are commonly referred to in the object-oriented world, and will give you a good working knowledge of both when to use those patterns in your own development efforts and how to use them effectively in Visual Basic.

How This Book Is Organized

The first part of this book deals with *design patterns*, a method of cataloging good design in application development. It also touches upon the way certain UML diagrams are used to catalog those patterns. The core of the book provides a catalog of various design patterns that can be used in your day-to-day design and development efforts. Each chapter uses the same basic outline:

- An introduction to the pattern

- A discussion (when necessary) of the different approaches to the pattern

- A UML diagram of the pattern and how it works

- Sample uses of the pattern, including the VB code that is used

- Other uses of the pattern
- A list of related patterns
- A conclusion

It is our hope that you will be able to use this book as a quick reference guide when you are considering a new piece of functionality for an application. The contents of this book should provide you with ideas for various ways to achieve functionality in your specific implementation.

Part 1: Introduction to Using UML and Design Patterns in Visual Basic

The first section of the book introduces UML, design patterns, and some basic techniques for how to use design patterns in Visual Basic. Chapter 1, "An Introduction to UML," provides a general overview of UML with a particular focus on the diagrams that are used in cataloging design patterns. Chapter 2, "An Introduction to Design Patterns," discusses the history of design patterns and the goals of this book, as compared to those of the book that began the discussion of this subject: *Design Patterns: Elements of Reusable Object-Oriented Software*, by Erich Gamma, Richard Helm, Ralph Johnson, John Vlissides, and Grady Booch. Finally, Chapter 3, "Visual Basic and Design Patterns," discusses some basic VB techniques, including implementing interfaces, that are useful in creating the patterns discussed in the book.

Part 2: Structural Patterns

The second part of the book discusses *structural patterns*, those design patterns that describe how objects interact with each other. In other words, these chapters focus on the architectural framework of the objects. We focus on seven architectural patterns: bridge, adapter, composite, decorator, facade, flyweight, and proxy.

A *bridge* pattern allows you to separate an interface from its implementation, so that the two can vary independently. You would use a bridge pattern when you want to vary the implementation of a particular method at run time, but you don't want to recompile the client code. This pattern also allows you to standardize an implementation across multiple classes by bridging all the interface classes to one implementation object.

The *adapter* pattern, also known as a *wrapper* pattern, allows two objects to communicate even though they have incompatible interfaces. Adapter accomplishes this by using an intermediary object that is compliant with the client object and delegates the execution of the client requests to the incompatible server object.

The *composite* pattern provides a unified interface that both collection classes and leaf node classes can inherit. By defining one interface, clients can treat items and collections uniformly within a hierarchy. Client code can recursively iterate through a part-whole hierarchy without having to write separate code to distinguish between the collections and primitives. The composite pattern eliminates the need to write case statements that depend on the type of class when traversing a hierarchy.

The *decorator* pattern allows you to assign additional responsibilities to an object without subclassing. It allows an object to add new functionality to another object dynamically. As a result, you can use the decorator pattern as an alternative to implementation inheritance. The decorator pattern encloses an object within a decorator object; this decorator object adds additional functionality without modifying the interface of the original object. Since the interface is not modified—and must be implemented completely by the decorator object—you can stack multiple decorators. This stacking provides layers of functionality that are added dynamically to a component.

The *facade* pattern provides a relatively simple interface to a complex subsystem or set of subsystems. Facade is used when a system provides its services through multiple subsystems or through calling multiple procedures. In order for clients to use the services of the system, they would have to be familiar with the intricacies of its subsystems and procedures. Facade shields clients from the intricacies of the subsystems by providing a simple interface for clients to call. In turn, the facade makes the necessary calls to its constituents to provide the service.

The *flyweight* pattern provides a method to pool and share a large number of contexts. It allows a single object to be used in several contexts simultaneously. This pattern allows you to design applications from an object-oriented view without the cost of instantiating a large number of objects, which could be prohibitive and inefficient.

The *proxy* pattern provides a surrogate object that delegates method calls to another object. It acts like a placeholder for an object that can be used to efficiently control access to the other object. The proxy mimics the other object to the extent that the client does not know that it is communicating with a proxy. The proxy pattern is used whenever you need an object to receive method calls on behalf of another object.

Part 3: Behavioral Patterns

Part 3 focuses on behavioral patterns, which describe how you can use objects to change the behavior of a system at run time. These are the most useful patterns to the VB developer, and we focus on twelve of these patterns: observer, mediator, chain of responsibility, command, interpreter, iterator, visitor, template, hook, memento, state, and strategy.

The *observer* pattern defines a one-to-many dependency between objects so that when one object changes state, all of its dependents are notified and updated automatically. There are two main types of observers: pull observers and push observers. The difference between the two is in how the observer relates to its subject or subjects. A pull observer is an active observer that pulls in the state of its subjects. In contrast to a pull observer, a push observer is a passive observer that needs its subjects to send notification messages in order for the observer to perform its role of updating a client.

The *mediator* pattern creates an object (the mediator) that acts like a traffic cop, controlling the interaction between a set of objects. The mediator encapsulates the rules of interaction between the set of objects. This is accomplished by loosely coupling the objects: the objects are not aware of each other; they are only aware of the mediator object. All "traffic" goes through the mediator.

The *chain of responsibility* pattern is an extremely flexible and extensible pattern. This pattern decouples the sender of a request from its receiver by giving more than one object a chance to handle the request. The request is passed along a group or "chain" of objects. Use the chain of responsibility pattern when more than one object can handle a request, but the requesting object does not know which object should answer the request.

The *command* pattern is used to turn a client procedure call into an object. Command gives the procedure request a life of its own so that it can have its own behaviors and properties. The command object does not carry out the request; rather it receives the request from the client, performs the functionality that it was designed to do, and then passes the request to the server object that is able to carry out the client's request. The command pattern allows you to add intelligence and behavior to procedure calls without modifying the client or server.

The *interpreter* pattern is used to help an application understand a natural language statement and execute the intended functionality of the statement. Interpreter-type functionality is used every day by developers in the form of code compilers and utilities that execute SQL statements. You can use many algorithms to provide this functionality; some algorithms provide good performance while others minimize resource consumption. The benefit of interpreter is in the flexibility it provides. It allows you to easily add new syntax rules and multiple implementations of a statement.

The *iterator* pattern provides a method to sequentially access members of a collection. This pattern separates the traversal mechanism and state management from an aggregate object. It removes the interface to traverse a group of objects from the aggregate object without revealing the underlying representation. Removing the mechanism to iterate through the collection allows different algorithms to be used to step through the collection (for example a forward iteration and a reverse iteration) without bloating the collection interface. In addition, the iterator pattern allows multiple clients to iterate through the same collection and be at different points.

The *visitor* pattern is used when operations must be performed upon numerous elements of an object model. Without the visitor, this type of functionality is usually implemented by spreading the required operations throughout the object model. Visitor provides a clean and more flexible model by abstracting the operations from the elements of the object model, and turning them into visitor objects. The visitor objects traverse the object model and perform their respective operations upon the individual elements. The visitor pattern allows you to keep an object model neat by abstracting into separate objects the operations which have to be performed on the elements of the model. It also allows you to easily add or remove operations without touching the elements of the model.

The *template method* pattern is a simple, yet fundamental, pattern for code reuse. The key to this pattern is putting the skeleton of an algorithm within a method (the template method). Steps in the algorithm become methods called from the template method. This keeps the overall algorithm constant, while allowing you to change how the individual steps of the algorithm are carried out. Template is best suited for when you are implementing a defined algorithm. It helps you avoid spaghetti code by standardizing the steps of the code first and then implementing each individual step.

The *hook* pattern allows developers in the future, after the original code has been written, to implement currently unforeseen functionality. A hook is simply a call from within a working procedure to an unimplemented procedure, meaning a procedure that consists of only the procedure stub without any implementation code. The call to the procedure is known as the hook and the empty procedure is known as the hook operation. The hook operation is where code for future functionality will be written.

The *memento* pattern is used when an object needs to record its current state so that it can be restored to that state at a later time. Memento is best suited for externalizing the state of an object when you can't—or don't want to—burden the originator with implementing the storing and restoration of state. In cases where you have to externalize protected data, the design of memento allows you to hide that data from the objects that handle it.

The *state* pattern allows an object's implementation to change at run time depending on the internal state of the object. It provides a way to alter the behavior of an object whenever the state of the object changes. To achieve this, the object delegates its behavior to encapsulated state-specific objects.

The *strategy* pattern abstracts a family of algorithms into individual objects that share a common interface so that they can be used interchangeably. A family of algorithms is a group of calculations that aim to solve the same problem in different ways. Strategy calls for the separate algorithms to be encapsulated in individual objects that conform to a common interface. The client is bound to the interface, and can be dynamically pointed to use any one of the individual strategy objects.

Part 4: Creational Patterns

The last part of our catalog deals with creational patterns, which are used when creating objects. Since Visual Basic is a high-level language, there are not too many choices to be made when creating objects, so there aren't too many creational patterns that are appropriate for the VB programmer. The final four chapters of the book focus on four that are factory, singleton, builder, and prototype.

The *factory* pattern provides a mechanism to separate a client from the process of creating a set of related objects or products. It provides an interface to delegate the creation of objects without specifying the concrete class. The factory encapsulates the rules for instantiating objects and buffers the client from the knowledge of the concrete class being instantiated.

The *singleton* pattern ensures that only one instance of a class exists at any time. It forces client applications to work with only one instance of a class and will not allow these applications to instantiate more than one instance. It provides a single, global point of access for clients to work with a resource.

The *builder* pattern provides a mechanism for building objects that allows the same interface to build different types of objects. Builder does this by separating the interface that builds the object from its implementation. This allows you to modify the implementation of a builder without breaking existing clients, and to easily add implementations that will be compatible with existing clients.

The *prototype* pattern provides a method to create objects by cloning pre-exisisting objects. It allows clients to create new objects, not by instantiating the object, but by asking another object—the prototype—to clone itself. By using the prototype pattern, you can internalize the instantiation and initialization of new objects into the class itself.

Appendices

Finally, we have provided three appendices at the end of the book.

Appendix A, "Recommended Books," provides a list of other books you may find useful. There is a list of books about design patterns for programming, a book on design patterns in architecture, and another list of books on UML. These lists are in no way exhaustive, but each book mentioned here rates at least four out of five stars in our personal listing, and we feel that each will be helpful in furthering your education on these topics.

Appendix B, "Recommended Web Sites," provides a list of Web sites that have interesting information on design patterns. There is an inexhaustible supply of information on the Web about patterns, and these sites will help you become familiar with this rich resource. In fact, each of these sites has links to dozens of others. We have attempted to provide a brief description of the site in the appendix in order to give you a place to start.

Appendix C, "List of Patterns," provides an overview of all of the design patterns listed in this book. You should use these to help you when you begin a search for a solution to a design problem. Use this appendix to get a best guess as to an appropriate pattern, and then go to the chapter on the specific pattern for more information, as well as a list of other patterns that may fit the bill.

About the Web Site

This book's Web site contains working versions of all of the code that is in the book. Whereas in the book we only showed the pieces of the code that demonstrated the pattern, on the Web site you can download the entire set of working code. Over time, as new versions of Visual Basic are released, the Web site will be enhanced with other code samples, new articles on patterns, and updates.

You can link to the code for this book on the Sybex Web site (`www.sybex.com`) and on the Flash Creative Management Web site (`www.flashcreative.com`).

About the Authors

Yair Alan Griver is a partner and Chief Information Officer at Flash Creative Management, a Hackensack, NJ–based business and technology consulting firm. Flash is a Microsoft Solution Provider and a Microsoft Authorized Technical Education Center.

Alan is responsible for overseeing the development of Flash's methods and its development frameworks. He has received the "Most Valuable Professional" award from Microsoft for his expertise in applying Microsoft technology to real world applications and for sharing that knowledge with other software developers.

Alan has written articles published in many leading publications, has lectured throughout the world on computer systems and software design, and has written five books on Visual FoxPro and Visual Basic. He can be reached at 201-489-2500 ext. 201 or at `alang@flashcreative.com`.

Matthew Arnheiter is a senior consultant for Flash Creative Management. He was a contributing author on *MCSD Test Success: Visual Basic 6 and Distributed Applications* (Sybex, 1999). He is also a monthly columnist for *Component Advisor* magazine. Matthew specializes in designing and building enterprise database and collaborative solutions. He can be reached at 201-489-2500 ext. 213 or `matta@flashcreative.com`.

Michael Gellis is a senior consultant at Flash Creative Management. He is responsible for Visual Basic and Internet-related software development. He co-authored *MCSD Test Success: Visual Basic 6 Distributed Applications* (Sybex, 1999).

He has also been published in several popular software development magazines. Michael has spoken at Microsoft's TechEd conference on the topic of Visual Basic and Design Patterns. He can be reached at 201-489-2500 ext. 276 or `mikeg@flash-creative.com`.

About Flash Creative Management

Flash Creative Management works with businesses to jointly map their strategies and to build the supporting processes and technology needed to achieve growth and profit objectives.

Flash Creative Management accomplishes this by supporting an exemplary professional and learning culture that attracts leading IT and strategic planning professionals and helps them develop their skills. Flash professionals have expertise in technology development, strategic planning, and process redesign.

Flash business projects have included aiding companies in strategic and tactical operational planning, planning of companies' Internet, intranet, and extranet strategies, providing project management expertise to a client's internal IT group, and redesigning the process for creating and selling new software products for a Fortune 500 company.

Flash's IT projects have included developing complete Web-based applications, which use component-based architectures based on VB and VFP, as well as SQL Server and Microsoft Site Server/E-Commerce Edition.

Flash's speaking engagements have included the W3C's European conference on XML and the Enterprise, Windows 2000 Connections, SQL Connections 2000, and Tech Ed.

To combine the needs of business with technology, Flash's team members are not only Microsoft Certified Professionals and Solution Developers, but also have an extensive set of project management skills.

Flash Creative Management's team members have written numerous journal articles and books about business strategy, Web site management, compensation planning, and the design and development of applications. Some of the books written by Flash Creative consultants include the following:

- *MCSD Test Success: Visual Basic 6 Distributed Applications* (Sybex, 1999)

- *Windows NT Workstation 4 Unleashed* (Sams, 1996)

- *The Visual FoxPro Codebook* (Sybex, 1995)
- *The FoxPro 2.6 Codebook* (Sybex, 1994)
- *The FoxPro Codebook* (Business One/Irwin, 1992)

For more information about our services, or to read some of the articles mentioned in the authors' bios, please visit Flash Creative's Web site at www.flashcreative.com.

Introduction

chapter 1

An Introduction to UML

- What is a modeling language?

- Why use UML and design patterns?

- A history of UML

- UML in the analysis phase of application development

- UML in the design phase of application development

Over the past four decades, the computer science industry has become increasingly more complex, and is evolving from an art form into a science. As part of this evolution, software engineering has progressed from having many incompatible modeling symbologies, toward a single widely accepted standard modeling language. This language uses standard diagrams that explain design decisions. In turn, these standard diagrams facilitate more efficient communication between teams of developers, enabling them to work together in solving larger problems.

With this greater complexity, component-based software development, in particular, requires standards for analyzing business problems, the approaches to solving those problems, and how those approaches are implemented. Component-based systems today have to be flexible to handle business changes and scalable to handle Web-based front-ends. In addition, they need to be easily understood so that new business initiatives can be implemented using existing components. Today, Unified Modeling Language (UML) is the standard modeling language for documenting the analysis and design of software systems. Design patterns facilitate the transfer of design decisions from one developer to another, and provide for standard approaches that add flexibility to systems.

What Is a Modeling Language?

The Unified Modeling Language is an extensible set of standard models used to analyze, design, and plan the deployment of an application. These models typically do not (and arguably should not) describe the implementation of the designs. Implementation is left up to developers. Communication between one developer and another is aided by *design patterns* , which are abstract solutions to recurring problems. Patterns are typically documented with various ways of implementing designs, and provide the pros and cons to various implementation decisions. The documentation of patterns typically includes various UML-based illustrations.

The relationship between a UML diagram and a design pattern is similar to that of an architectural blueprint of a house and the type of windows placed in that house. When you build a house, you begin with a basic idea of what you and your family want and call in a contractor to get information about price and looks. Once you have signed off on the basic diagram, the contractor handles the hiring of specialists and the creation of diagrams that are specific to their needs (like electrical and plumbing schematics). These diagrams are equivalent to both the basic and the more detailed diagrams available to UML.

Your job does not end there, however. You can select many different types of windows, for instance, that all fit within the same size hole in the wall. There are pros and cons to each type of window; some are easier to clean, some are less expensive. You decide which type of window to install based on your needs. This is similar to using a pattern to decide which coding decisions to make based on certain needs. This book focuses on the patterns used in Visual Basic applications and discusses the pros and cons of using them.

Why Use UML and Patterns?

The simple answer is because you have to *plan* your implementation. This is true whether you are beginning to tackle larger applications with Visual Basic, or whether you are starting to use VB and COM's capabilities together to create component based systems. UML allows you to document any design decisions you make, and to test various approaches to class design before you write any code. UML can also be used to document the system after you've built it, or to document an existing system.

Patterns allow you to use well-defined and accepted architectures to create flexible components. These components, in turn, are more easily understood, reused, and extended. The combination of a pattern and associated UML diagrams, will not only allow a team of developers to work together on a good design, but will also document and standardize approaches to future enhancements of the system.

This chapter provides an overview of the UML diagrams and discusses how UML fits into the analysis and design effort. Some of the UML diagrams (particularly the class and sequence diagrams) will be used throughout this book to visually show how the patterns we discuss work and are implemented.

A Brief History of UML

Designing an application is a complex task. And, as applications became more complex, software engineers developed certain standards—called *methodologies*—

for analyzing business problems and designing software solutions. These methodologies include the following:

- Object Modeling Technique (OMT) by James Rumbaugh
- Booch Method by Grady Booch
- Object-Oriented Software Engineering (OOSE) by Ivar Jacobson
- Coad-Yourdon by Peter Coad and Ed Yourdon
- Class Responsibility Collaboration (CRC) by Rebecca Wirfs-Brock

In the mid-nineties, the three authors of OMT, Booch, and OOSE began to work together (as part of Rational Software) on unifying their methods, calling the result the Unified Modeling Language (UML). UML provides system architects working on object analysis and design with one consistent language for specifying, visualizing, constructing, and documenting the artifacts of software systems, as well as for business modeling. The Object Management Group (OMG) certified UML as an industry standard in 1997. Since that time, many corporations and tool vendors have adopted UML as a standard approach for software analysis and design. As a standard, more tools will begin to support UML and will be able to interoperate through these diagrams.

UML in Application Development

The five basic phases of application development are:

- Analysis
- Design
- Construction
- Testing
- Deployment

In this chapter, we will explore the analysis and design phases because they use special diagrams specific to each phase. On the other hand, during the construction phase, you do not create new UML diagrams per se. Rather, you write code using classes based on the diagrams created in the analysis and design phases. Likewise, although you can use standard UML diagrams in the testing phase, there are no special diagrams specific to that phase. The testing phase uses the documents from the other phases and ensures that the diagrams are adhered to and are correct. The deployment diagrams deal with how we're going to combine classes into DLLs and what servers and workstations we'll be using. As a result, they do not apply to the concept of design patterns that deal with the architecture of our classes. A study of the analysis and design phases will provide you with a thorough background in the use of UML for design patterns.

NOTE   This chapter provides a brief overview of UML so that VB developers who do not have a deep knowledge of UML will understand the diagrams in this book. For an in-depth discussion of UML, see *UML Distilled: Applying the Standard Object Modeling Language*, by Fowler and Scott (ISBN 0-201-32563-2).

The Analysis Phase

Analysis, the first phase of application development, translates a set of business processes into a standardized language that you can use in prototyping and designing classes and database models. UML defines two standard models used in the analysis phase: *use cases* and *sequence diagrams*. A use case is a graphical and textual representation of a single process. A use case divides the process into the *basic case* (which occurs most of the time) and the *secondary cases* (which fall out of the basic case). It focuses on the trigger for a process and what occurs during the process. The use case can be used for both describing a business process and the steps a user takes in a system. It is this duality of roles that makes the use case the link between a business issue and the start of the system analysis process.

The *sequence diagram* focuses on the interaction between the players in a use case. It describes what information is passed from one player to another, and what requests one player makes to another. This diagram is also used in class design, and can be used as a bridge from analysis to design. Early versions of a sequence diagram do not discuss system internals, but rather basic messages from one player to another. As you move into design, you begin fleshing out the details of the objects in the sequence and the parameters passed to the various methods.

The Use Case Model

One of the best ways to capture the overall system functionality is through a *use-case* model. The use-case model uses a concept known as *actors* (not necessarily users!) to help visualize what is outside the system, and a concept known as use case to define what should be performed by the system. Let's take a more detailed look at the various parts of a use case.

Business Use Cases vs. System Use Cases

At our company, we like to think that there are two types of use cases: *business use cases* and *system use cases*. The former is used to capture the intent of the business process. A business use case, then, is directed towards the business people for whom we are designing the software solution. It discusses the processes that people go through to accomplish something and does not assume the use of any technology. For instance, a business use case for a catalog order might include the following steps:

Provide the customer identification.

1. Provide the list of items to be ordered.

2. Confirm the credit card number.

3. Confirm the order.

4. Confirm the ship-to address.

The system use case, on the other hand, is often tied to a software prototype and describes how the business process is accomplished through technology. The system use case is used to capture the steps in the software, and describes what the software will act or look like. The business use case may be divided into multiple system use cases that, for example, separately discuss the interface for a Windows-based system and an automated telephone-based order entry system. This is how we begin to move our model from a business process to software analysis.

The Actor

The actor triggers a use case or is needed during the action of a use case. Note that we differentiate between an actor and a user. This distinction indicates that an actor may not necessarily be a human being sitting at a terminal interacting with the system. It could, in fact, be an external device connected to one of the computer's ports, even another computer. When an actor does represent an individual user, however, it is important to remember that the actor represents the *role* that the user is playing, rather than the individual.

You can gain insight into the difference between an actor and a user by applying object-oriented concepts. Think of an actor as a class and an individual user as an *instance* of that class. Instances only exist when the user does something with the system. With this approach, it becomes easier to see that the same person can appear as instances of several different actors.

For example, in a very small company, one individual's job may be to input customer orders into the system. That same individual may also be responsible for going into the warehouse and filling the customer order by placing the ordered items in a shipping carton (and then mailing the order to the customer). There are two distinct actors here: the order-entry person and the shipper. Creating a use-case model with a single actor may cause us to design the system incorrectly—perhaps missing some required functionality—thereby resulting in a system that the user is not satisfied with. By using the actor concept instead of a user concept, it is easier to discover all the different ways in which the system will be used. In the use-case model, the actor is represented by the symbol in Figure 1.1.

FIGURE 1.1
The symbol for an actor that is representing a user

User

The Use Case

According to Ivar Jacobson in *Object-Oriented Software Engineering*, when an actor uses the system, he or she initiates "a behaviorally related sequence of transactions." This sequence is called a use case. An example of a use case is "Input customer order." It is important to note that at this point, we are not concerned with exactly how this use case will be implemented in the system. Instead, we will focus on what must happen for the use case to be considered complete by creating a use-case description.

You can apply object-oriented concepts to the use-case concept as well. Think of the use-case description as the class and each use case as an instance of that class. When an actor performs an action on the system, an instance of some use case is created, and the transaction belonging to that use case (defined in the use-case description) is executed. A use case, then, represents some type of behavior in the system, and this behavior has a state (how far the behavior has reached, what the status of the system is, and so on). Even though a use case represents a behavior, it is useful to think of a use case as an object (an instance of a use-case description). The use case is represented in the use-case model shown in Figure 1.2.

FIGURE 1.2
The symbol for a
hypothetical use case,
"Making a Phone Call"

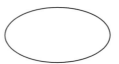

Making a phone call

When pinpointing use cases, it is important to determine the *intent* of the user's actions. For example, as part of his normal daily activities, a user may be notified of a problem with a particular customer, call the customer for notification, fill out a specific form, and send the form out for approval. Just by looking at this description, however, you cannot tell that the intent of these actions is to process overdrawn balances. Only once you determine this intent, then, can you create a use case for it, as shown in Figure 1.3.

FIGURE 1.3
A sample use-case
interaction

Teller   Process Overdrawn Balances

Because of the high-level nature of this "Process overdrawn balances" use case, it can be thought of as a kind of container, or a *use envelope* , as it were; the intent of the use case is written on the outside of the envelope. The details of how the intent is accomplished, in terms of other use cases, scenarios, and even other use envelopes, are kept inside the envelope, and can be seen in the use-case description.

NOTE   It is important to capture the intent of each use case because it is unlikely to change over time, even though the underlying design may change. The entire set of use-case intents and use-case descriptions comprise the functionality of a system. As a result, the use-case model provides a simple, yet effective, means for communicating functional requirements to system users.

A Sample Use Case Model

Let's create a simple use case model—involving a pay telephone—that mirrors something in real life. There are a number of basic processes involving pay telephones, including:

- Making a phone call

- Fixing an out-of-order phone

- Emptying change from the phone

Each of these processes becomes part of the *use envelope* . The use envelope is detailed as a single diagram that shows the overall uses for a pay telephone, as shown in Figure 1.4.

FIGURE 1.4
The Payphone Use
Envelope

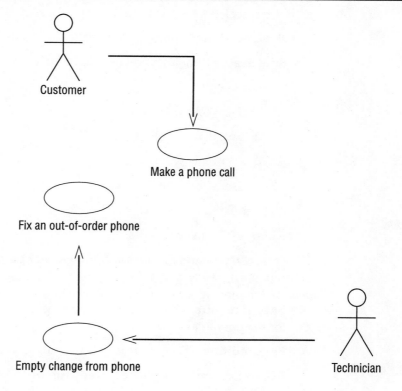

Figure 1.4 shows that two actors are required to fulfill all the use cases associated with a pay phone: customer and technician. The customer is only involved in making a phone call, and the technician is involved in both fixing and emptying the phone. Fixing an out-of-order phone only happens as a result of emptying the phone. A phone is fixed only when a technician notices, while emptying it, that it is out of order. Note that by showing that fixing the phone is an extension of emptying it, we preclude the possibility of a customer notifying the phone company of the problem. When reviewing the use envelope, someone may notice this omission, allowing us to modify the use envelope appropriately. This is a case where having a diagram in addition to text allows us to see things from a higher level, catching analysis errors more quickly.

Each use case in the envelope is described textually as well as graphically. Figure 1.4 provides a representation of the entire system. The text gives a description of each use case. Let's take a look at one of the use cases from the above model.

Use case name: Making a phone call.

Brief description: User makes a phone call to another party.

Flow of events:

1. User picks up receiver.

2. User deposits change for call.

3. User dials phone.

4. User speaks on phone.

5. User hangs up.

Alternative flow of events:

2a. User enters phone card number and password to pay for call.

4a. Other party does not answer.

Special requirements: There is a working telephone and a means of paying for the phone call.

Pre-conditions: The phone is not currently in use.

Post-conditions: The phone is ready for use by another.

The Sequence Diagram

Once you define and model your case, you can create *sequence diagrams* for any of the use cases that you'd like to see in more detail. Sequence diagrams focus on the interactions over time between the various objects in a use case. Using a sequence diagram for a system use case allows you to see the messages that go between your objects. These messages then make up the public interface of your classes. Figure 1.5 shows the sequence diagram for the Making a Phone Call use case.

Remember, the sequence diagrams exist in both analysis and design, and once you have created a complete sequence diagram, you are probably in design. The design phase is where you begin exploring which patterns you can use to implement that design. To look at it another way, the system's design is made up of various design fragments (portions of the design). You use patterns when you code selected design fragments.

FIGURE 1.5
A sequence diagram of
Making a Phone Call

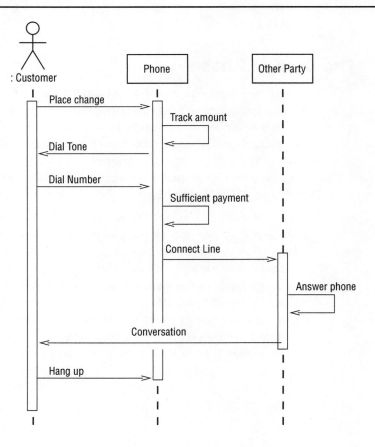

As you can see in Figure 1.5, there are three objects that make up the use case: the customer, the phone, and the other party. By reading the diagram from top to bottom, you can see that although the customer interacts with the phone for the entire process, the other party is involved only if there is sufficient payment and the line is connected.

NOTE   We will be using more sequence diagrams throughout this book to detail the communication between various objects in patterns.

The use-case and sequence UML diagrams are used during the analysis phase to describe the business processes and interactions between the objects in the business. The UML diagram mediates between a process view and system view of an application, although the sequence diagram begins the process of viewing the system as a series of messages between objects. This gives some idea about the life span of an object.

The Design Phase

Design, the second phase of development, consists of translating analysis documents—including use case scenarios—into more detailed models. Developers then use these models to create applications that will help businesses run their processes. In addition, since the models are standardized, developers can use tools to begin the creation of the application. For instance, Microsoft Visual Modeler, a modeling tool that ships with Visual Basic, will automatically generate the skeletons of VB classes based on the class diagrams in the model.

UML defines a number of standard models that are useful in the design. We'll be focusing on two of them: *class diagrams,* which detail the properties and methods of a class, and *activity diagrams,* which are used to map out the inner workings of a method or property. Class diagrams show both the hierarchy of classes in an object-oriented system and also how various classes interact with each other to accomplish their tasks. We will be using class diagrams and activity diagrams to show the underlying properties, methods of classes, and how some of the internal methods of classes work. As we mentioned earlier, we'll also be using some sequence diagrams to show how objects in a pattern work together to accomplish their tasks. Finally, we'll use state diagrams to show how the state of an object changes during a particular course of events. For now, let's take a closer look at class and activity diagrams.

NOTE The relationship between Visual Basic and object orientation are discussed in Chapter 3, "Visual Basic and Design Patterns."

The Class Diagram

A class diagram provides a static picture of the classes in a system and their relationships to other classes. Class diagrams consist of a box that details a class and various types of arrows that detail relationships. Let's take a look at the pieces of a class diagram.

The Class

A class is shown as a square box with three sections. The top section shows the class name, the middle section shows the properties of the class, and the bottom section shows the methods in the class. Properties and methods show their visibility (public, private, and friend) on the left side of the name. Optionally, properties can show initial values on the right and methods can show their parameters (with their types) and return values, also on the right. An example of this diagram can be seen in Figure 1.6.

The method description detailed in UML will look something like this:

```
Method1(Param1:Integer = 5, Param2:String):Boolean
```

The previous line tells us that a method, called Method1, takes two parameters, and returns a Boolean. The two parameters are called Param1 and Param2. Param1 is an integer with a default value of 5 and Param2 is a string with no default value.

Bringing the method description into the proper section of the class box, gives us a completed class diagram. Figure 1.6 shows a sample customer class.

FIGURE 1.6

A sample customer class

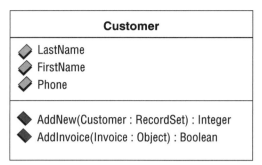

The sample customer class in Figure 1.6 shows three public properties and two public methods. The properties simply store information about the class; in our case last name, first name, and phone. The AddNew() public method takes a recordset and returns an integer. The AddInvoice public method takes an object and returns a Boolean. Now that you have an understanding of the classes themselves, let's take a look at how to connect them.

Linking Classes

UML defines to link classes in four ways: association, aggregation, dependency, and generalization. The three most commonly used in class diagrams are detailed as follows:

Association   A plain line is used to link two classes in a relationship. In association, each class can exist without the other, but they do work together to achieve the goal illustrated in the diagram.

Aggregation   Aggregation is shown by a line with a diamond on one side. Aggregation describes the "has a" relationship between classes. For instance, an invoice "has a" line item. In this case, one class (line item) cannot exist without the other (invoice). The diamond is placed on the class that contains the other class.

Generalization   This relationship is also known as the inheritance relationship. Generalization specifies that one class descends from another, where the more specialized child is substitutable for the more general parent. The child has the same properties, methods, and capabilities as the parent. Generalization is displayed as a line with a triangle pointing to the class that it is inherited from. This relation is less useful in a VB design, due to VB's lack of implementation inheritance. We will use aggregation to simulate inheritance.

A Sample Class Diagram

Figure 1.7 shows a sample class diagram for a simple customer invoicing system. This figure shows how a customer class works with the invoice class. The invoice class contains line items in an aggregation relationship. Also shown is the fact that all of the concrete classes (customer, invoice, and line item) inherit capabilities from the AbstractBizObj class (which could have the capability of reading and writing to a database in a standard manner, error handling, etcetera).

FIGURE 1.7
A customer invoicing class
diagram

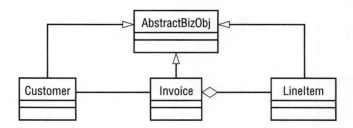

Now that you've seen how to model classes in the static form of the sample class diagram, let's take a look at the activity diagram for the same business process.

The Activity Diagram

Activity diagrams are used to detail the more complex methods of objects. Activity diagrams, as shown in Figure 1.8, are similar to flow charts and focus on the decision points in any single action. They consist of the following elements:

Starting point   Represented by a filled in circle.

End point   Represented by a filled in circle with a circle around it.

Activities   Represented by rounded rectangles. Numerous activities are connected by arrows that show movement through the procedure.

Decision points   Represented by diamonds. Decision points provide paths for various decisions.

FIGURE 1.8
A sample activity diagram
for posting an invoice

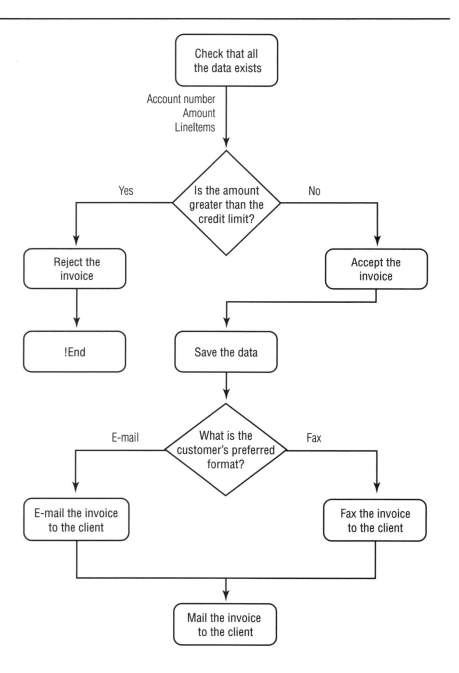

As we can see from Figure 1.8, posting an invoice requires checking that all the necessary data exists, verifying that the invoice amount is not greater than the customer credit limit, saving the data, and mailing, e-mailing, or faxing an invoice, depending on the available customer information.

Conclusion

UML consists of a number of models that are used in the analysis, design, and deployment phases of development. We have found UML to be particularly useful in the analysis and design phases, with a particular emphasis on use case, sequence, class, and activity diagrams. This book, which emphasizes standardized solutions to recurring problems, will focus on the sequence, class, and activity diagrams that describe patterns and their methods.

chapter 2

An Introduction to Design Patterns

■ What are design patterns?

■ The history of design patterns

■ The basics of design patterns

■ Types of design patterns

■ Using UML with design patterns

"As you go from the living room to the dining room, you pass through an arch."

What did you picture in your mind as you read that sentence? Most of you probably pictured going from a room with a sofa to a room with a table, without having to use a door. I didn't have to describe the dimensions or furniture in either room, nor did I discuss the angle of the arch, its load bearing capabilities, the materials used, but you did have a picture in your mind. The sentence about passing through the arch uses three common patterns that you are familiar with from your day-to-day life. A few words conjured up very complex pictures, as well as an understanding of the architecture of the house. Furthermore, to an architect, the image of the arch brings to mind various equations and formulae that can be used to calculate things like height, load bearing capabilities, and material usage. The term arch is a common architectural design pattern.

Application developers can make use of design patterns as well. *Design patterns* give us a way of naming and describing abstract solutions across a range of recurring problems. They allow class designers and developers to speak the same language, reducing the amount of time spent scribbling on a white board, and allow for better application development.

This book is all about patterns. Each chapter discusses one common pattern that you will find in your application's code. We hope that by recognizing these patterns, you'll be able to design flexibility into your applications on purpose. In other words, instead of stumbling over a good way of doing something, you'll be able to say to yourself "I know I need flexibility here, what pattern should I use?" This book will help answer that question, and provide the model and code for those patterns, giving you a head start on using good coding practices.

NOTE   Although Design Patterns are often achieved using *inheritance*, they are always based on *object referencing*. Even though Visual Basic does not support inheritance, by using VB's IMPLEMENTS keyword to standardize an interface, and by using object referencing, we are able to create VB versions of patterns that give us the same flexibility. We discuss these approaches in Chapter 3, "Creating Patterns Using Visual Basic.

This chapter introduces the concept of design patterns, discusses how the concept of design patterns started, and why design patterns are getting so much mind share in the programming world.

What Are Design Patterns?

The two words that make up this method of application development—design and pattern—merit contemplation. The dictionary provides the literal definition of each word. Merriam-Webster's Collegiate Dictionary, Tenth Edition, defines *pattern* as:

- "a form or model proposed for imitation"
- "a discernible coherent system based on the intended interrelationship of component parts"

It defines *design* as:

- "deliberate purposive planning"
- "a mental project or scheme in which means to an end are laid down"
- "a preliminary sketch or outline showing the main features of something to be executed"

In other words, a *design pattern* is a recurring, planned, solution that works across a range of problems. Throughout this book, as we identify these design patterns and give them names, we can begin to discuss design issues at a higher level, enabling faster design and a better understanding of the problem.

Let's look at two examples of discussions between two developers, to see where patterns can help out:

Scenario One:

"Since we want to separate out our approach to data access, I was thinking of creating a set of `behavior` classes that would standardize our access to data. I could have an `AbstractBehavior` class, which would have methods like "Next," "Prior," etcetera, and then subclass it to `TableBehavior` and `ViewBehavior` classes. Our business classes would call these methods from their methods of the same names."

"How would that work?"

"Well, our `bizobj` class would take a property called `oBehavior` which would contain a reference to an object which actually performs the data manipulation.

We could change the behavior of the data handling simply by instantiating a different subclass of `AbstractBehavior` and placing that in the `oBehavior` property. Get it?"

"Not totally, can you draw it out for me?"

"Hang on, I'll get a napkin."

Scenario Two:

"Since we want to separate out our approach to data access, I was thinking of creating a simple bridge pattern between behavior and business classes."

"Why not use an aggregate bridge?"

"We typically use only one behavior on data for an application, so there's no need to loop through different types. We can always replace the simple bridge for business objects that need a different one."

"You're right."

As you can see, the second scenario is much shorter, you don't need a napkin, and (assuming you understand the concept of a bridge pattern) delivers more information in a shorter amount of time. The developers in the second scenario can limit their discussion to architectural issues (what type of bridge to use), instead of explaining the code involved.

Patterns are all about architectures, their components, collaborations, and contracts. They allow developers to rise above code and discuss the best way to architect their applications. They are all about making applications more flexible when necessary.

Please note that patterns are not a silver bullet, although people sometimes speak of them as if they are. Their main purpose is to allow you to intelligently design applications and subsystems, deciding on the proper type of flexibility to provide. They are best used *after* you have an understanding of the business issues.

Patterns are also best used where flexibility is required. The more flexibility you build into an application, subsystem, or framework, the more training will be required for any new developers who want to understand the application that you are building. It is important to decide where flexibility is needed, then decide which pattern is best used in that place. With that said, let's begin with the history and basic structure of design patterns.

The History of Design Patterns

As mentioned above, software developers study design patterns to allow our applications to be more flexible, and we name them in order to make it easier for us to discuss our designs. Where does the concept of design patterns come from? This section discusses the history of design patterns.

Architecture and Design Patterns

Architect Christopher Alexander first detailed design patterns, and has since used them as a method for describing the best practices in architecture, and as a means for standardizing good design. In his article, "Toward a Personal Workplace," Alexander discusses the design patterns for a positive personalized workspace. Alexander first outlines the rules behind good personalized workspaces:

- People have a right to expect an emotionally enriching workplace environment.
- It is possible, with materials and methods already available, to achieve this environment.
- The actual cost is not significantly greater than what it costs to create an oppressive work environment.

In his book, *A Pattern Language: Towns, Buildings, Construction*, Alexander builds upon these principles, and describes various patterns that relate to these goals:

- Office Connections
- Flexible Office Space
- Small Work Groups
- Half-Private Offices

He also details other goals. Each of these patterns describes a way of designing the space and architecture that is required to attain the goal of a good personalized workspace.

Computer Science and Design Patterns

In 1995, with the publication of the book *Design Patterns* by Gamma, Helm, Johnson, and Vlissides, also known as the "Gang of Four," computer scientists began to discuss software design patterns. They applied the ideas behind Alexander's patterns in a book that detailed various programming patterns. The book also discusses when these programming patterns are needed. *Design Patterns* contains a catalog of patterns for object-oriented languages (with examples in Smalltalk and C++). Since then, various conferences and newsgroups have arisen to discuss and document further patterns. These patterns have usually been developed in C++.

Visual Basic developers interested in design patterns have sometimes been frustrated that useful examples of design patterns are typically limited to C++. The goal of this book is to show the Visual Basic developer how design patterns can be used in their application development efforts. To achieve this goal, we base most of our patterns on the same ones listed in the Gang of Four book. In so doing, we hope that the common language of UML will allow those working in Visual Basic, Visual C++, Java, Visual FoxPro—and indeed all developers—to communicate with each other more effectively.

The Basics of Design Patterns

One of the keys of object-oriented development, in fact any developments, is reuse. Most of the work on reuse has focused on reusing code. Design patterns allow you to reuse designs. In this way, you can create a standard interface for your components, reusing them as necessary wherever a similar interface is available. You end up programming to the interface of a class, component, or subsystem, instead of to its implementation. This allows you to use polymorphism on a higher level.

Object-oriented programming languages allow you to inherit from superclasses, automatically gaining any of their capabilities. This is known as *design time reuse*, since the inheritance tree is decided upon during design and development. Design patterns commonly focus on another method of reuse called *composition*. Using composition, one object has a reference to another object or multiple objects, and the ways in which they work together form the pattern. This is a *run time reuse*, since you can change the object references while the application is running.

Visual Basic does not support inheritance (as discussed in Chapter 3, "Visual Basic and Design Patterns") but it definitely supports object referencing and composition. This book will show how Visual Basic's capabilities can be used to create versions of patterns that work within the language, despite the lack of inheritance. Each chapter of the book will cover one pattern, discuss its use, and give a simple example of that use in Visual Basic. We will also be providing a Web site with all the sample code, as well as a larger example of many of the patterns in use in a running application.

A pattern has the following four essential elements:

Pattern name   Allows developers to discuss patterns in an easy manner without getting into the specifics of the code

Problem   Describes when it makes sense to use a pattern

Solution   Describes the object designs and collaborations that solve a problem

Consequences   Details the trade-off involved in the solution and points to additional patterns (with other consequences) that may be helpful as well

Design Pattern Groupings

In the Gamma, Helm book, design patterns were divided into three basic groups:

Creational patterns   Used when creating objects. Since Visual Basic is a high level language, many of the issues in object creation that appear in lower level languages do not usually affect the VB programmer. This book will focus on four creational patterns: *factory, builder, singleton,* and *prototype.*

Structural patterns   Describe how objects interact with each other. In other words, they focus on the architectural framework of the objects. We will be focusing on seven structural patterns: *bridge, adapter, composite, decorator, facade, flyweight,* and *proxy.*

Behavioral patterns   Describe how you can use objects to change the behavior of a system at run time. These are the most useful patterns to the VB developer, and we will focus on twelve of these behavioral patterns: *mediator, chain of responsibility, command, interpreter, iterator, visitor, template, hook, memento, observer, state,* and *strategy.*

We have selected the patterns that are most commonly used by VB developers, as well as those that are of most use to VB developers. As a result, we have focused on behavioral and structural patterns that can give the VB-based application the most flexibility when revisions are required.

Using UML with Design Patterns

In Chapter 1, "An Introduction to UML," we described various diagrams used to describe classes, objects, and how they interact with each other. It is this capability of objects to interact that we use in pattern definition.

When describing a pattern, it often helps to show how the various objects interact, as well as the class design for those objects. The patterns in this book will be defined using UML diagrams, including the *class*, *sequence*, and *activity* diagrams.

Because these are patterns, the various design options show up most clearly in a diagram format, rather than code. Code tends to be too verbose and implementation-specific to describe the solution, and is most useful when it illustrates an understood solution, rather than trying to show the solution itself. Therefore, this book will explain the patterns using UML, and will then show examples from an application that uses the patterns in this book.

As an example, let's go back to the discussion between the two programmers at the beginning of this chapter. For ease of reading, we'll duplicate the discussion here:

"Since we want to separate out our approach to data access, I was thinking of creating a set of `behavior` classes that would standardize our access to data. I could have an `AbstractBehavior` class, which would have methods like "Next," "Prior," etcetera, and then subclass it to `TableBehavior` and `ViewBehavior` classes. Our business classes would call these methods from their methods of the same names."

"How would that work?"

"Well, our `bizobj` class would take a property called `oBehavior`, which would contain a reference to an object that actually performs the data manipulation. We could change the behavior of the data handling simply by instantiating a different subclass of `AbstractBehavior` and placing that in the `oBehavior` property. Get it?"

"Not totally, can you draw it out for me?"

"Hang on, I'll get a napkin."

Picture what would be drawn on the napkin. In most cases, a picture of some sort will be drawn, in order to illustrate the point, as shown in Figure 2.1. It is possible that a few lines of code would also be written to emphasize a key point. UML provides standard diagrams and notes that can be used to do exactly this. That is why we will be using the various UML diagrams in each chapter. Look at how figure 2.1 illustrates the above issue discussed by the programmers. We have two possible Behavior classes (TableBehavior and ViewBehavior), either of which can be called by the BizObj class through its object reference (oBehavior).

FIGURE 2.1
A UML class diagram from
our example discussion

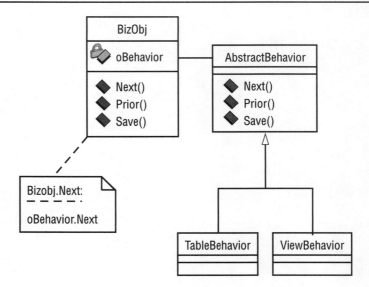

Conclusion

Patterns are most useful during class design when you want to add flexibility to a section of your design. The basic approach is to understand the business problem, design the business classes, and then decide where flexibility will be needed in the future. Once you've detailed those sections of your design, decide which patterns make the most sense for that type of flexibility.

When discussing a design decision with a colleague, design patterns offer common names for complex decisions, allowing you to cut to the chase, as it were, and have a discussion about the decision, without spending time explaining the details of that decision. It is this higher level approach that makes patterns so useful.

The next chapter will cover some of the basics for implementing patterns in Visual Basic, and the following chapters will each contain one useful pattern, its makeup, UML diagrams, and sample code to implement it.

chapter 3

Creating Patterns Using Visual Basic

- Inheritance and design patterns

- Understanding roles and implementations

- Implementing decoupled objects with Visual Basic

- Using the Implements keyword

Visual Basic developers will find using design patterns extremely useful in developing their applications. Design patterns are used to structure the interaction of objects. As a result, they are geared for object-based systems built with class modules. In addition, though, if a non-object-based system—such as one based on standard modules—is modularly designed so that its functions are clearly abstracted one from another, then it, too, can use some patterns. This book will closely examine the use of design patterns with object-based systems because Visual Basic developers will find that of the most value.

Inheritance and Design Patterns

Visual Basic developers may be daunted by popular design pattern documentation that uses inheritance to illustrate patterns. The truth is that inheritance and design patterns serve different purposes. Inheritance aids developers in creating an application, while design patterns aid the developer in designing the application.

Inheritance aids a developer during design time by reducing the amount of code needed to create an application. Using inheritance, a developer can create base classes that provide the basic functionality of an application. They can also reuse and modify that functionality by subclassing the base class. Inheritance also eases the modification and maintenance of an application by allowing a developer to modify a base class. The modification is automatically propagated to all subclasses. These capabilities of inheritance aid a developer during design time in creating an application.

In contrast, design patterns aid the developer in designing the architecture of a system by guiding the interaction of its objects. Granted that building with the tool of inheritance has its benefits. However the use or non-use of the tool does not affect whether one can create an application using the architectural tool of design patterns.

NOTE   Although Visual Basic does support interface inheritance using the `Implements` keyword, as described in the following sections, it does not support implementation inheritance, which allows subclasses to use functionality coded into parent classes.

Understanding Roles & Implementations

The power of design patterns is in their ability to dynamically guide the interactions of objects. The key to this ability is twofold: first, in the definition of roles, and second, in the separation of those roles from their implementation. In the following sections, we will discuss what roles and implementations are, how they benefit design patterns, and how to create patterns with Visual Basic.

Defining Roles & Implementations

A *role* is an object's responsibility in a system. Its responsibility is made up of the services it provides within the system. An object's *implementation* is how the object actually carries out its role. For example, consider an object that is used to display information to the user through a message box. It has a role and an implementation. Its role is to publish. It implements its role by displaying the information in a message box.

A role should be independent of its implementation, so that you can change the implementation without affecting the role. For example, let's say we choose to have the object send the information in an e-mail instead of displaying it in a message box. Its implementation changes, but its role remains the same. This example illustrates the difference between a role and an implementation and how the implementation can change without affecting the role.

Tightly Coupled versus Loosely Coupled Objects

Design patterns basically guide the interaction of objects, and allow objects to alter their implementation without affecting other objects in the system that interact with them. How can an object change its implementation without affecting the objects that interact with it? By having the other objects in the system depend upon the object's role and not upon its implementation.

To illustrate this point, let's use the publisher example used above. Let's say we have another object called Subject that gathers the pertinent information and then sends it to the Publisher object, which in turn publishes it in a message box. Suppose that Subject depends on the fact that Publisher displays the information modally, because it knows that Publisher implements its role by displaying a message box. If we were to change the implementation of Publisher to send the information in an e-mail, we'd break the Subject class. If, however, Subject knew nothing of Publisher's implementation, then we would be able to change Publisher without affecting Subject.

This example illustrates the difference between *tightly coupled objects* and *loosely coupled objects*. When object A depends on object B's implementation, then they are tightly coupled. This is a nice way of saying they are inflexible. When object A knows only of object B's *role* but not its *implementation*, then it is loosely coupled. This means that object B's implementation can be changed without affecting object A. The key to allowing objects to dynamically alter their functionality without breaking other objects, then, is by designing loosely coupled objects. Designing loosely coupled objects is the essence of design patterns.

Very Loosely Coupled Objects

Objects can even be decoupled to a further degree to allow for *dynamic object substitution*. In some patterns, multiple objects provide different implementations for one role. In these cases, the system dynamically sets which implementation object executes the role. To accomplish this, the client object must be bound to the role and not to a specific object. In these cases, the server and client objects are *very loosely coupled*; they aren't even bound to each other. This method of arranging objects is what gives design patterns the power of dynamic object substitution. Before we discuss how to do this in VB, we must first discuss how roles are defined.

Roles and Interfaces

An object's role is physically defined by its *public interface*. The public interface of an object is made up of its public procedures that client objects can call. Using our example of the Publisher object, the Publisher object would have a public interface consisting of one method called Publish that has one parameter called Information. This public interface is what defines its role as a Publisher. When a client object only knows the public interface of a server object, but not the implementation, then the client and server objects are at the first level of being loosely coupled. If the client object is bound to the public interface of the server object—but not to a specific implementation of the server object—then they have reached a greater level of separation.

Implementing Decoupled Objects with Visual Basic

Implementing the first level of loosely coupled objects requires you to design your objects so that they are oblivious to how a server object implements its role. Attaining the second level of loosely coupled objects is a bit more complicated. It involves defining *abstract interfaces*, *concrete classes,* and using the `Implements` keyword.

Abstract Interfaces and Concrete Classes

An abstract interface is a regular class module that contains all the public procedures that make up an object's public interface. It contains only procedure declarations but not any code for implementation. Client objects can bind directly to an abstract interface.

A *concrete class* is a class module that implements an abstract interface by providing the code that executes the procedures declared in the interface. Typically you will have several concrete classes that implement the interface in varying ways. In order for a concrete class to fulfill the role of an abstract interface, it must support all of the procedures declared by the interface. This *compliance to a uniform interface* is enforced with the `Implements` keyword, as explained below in "Using the `Implements` Keyword."

Client objects that are bound to the interface call the procedures of the interface, without necessarily knowing which concrete class will actually execute the procedure. The system dynamically sets which concrete class will implement the interface. This method of *dynamic object substitution* allows the system to dynamically alter the implementation of a role without breaking client objects.

Using the `Implements` Keyword

The `Implements` keyword is the glue that brings all this together. Here's how it works. The first step is to create an *abstract interface*. The abstract interface should contain all the procedures required by its role as explained above. The next step is to create concrete classes that implement the interface in different ways. This is done by adding class modules to the project and writing the `Implements` keyword, followed by the name of the interface in the Declarations section of the class.

This will do two things. First, it will add all of the procedures from the interface into the code window of the subclass. You must put code into every one of those procedures or else a compiler error will be raised. This forces all the concrete classes to conform to a uniform interface that is defined by the abstract class.

Second, and most important, it allows the subclass to be referenced as the interface's type. A variable declared as the interface's type can contain a reference to the subclass. As a result, a client can be bound to the abstract interface and the system can set that reference to point to any one of the concrete classes. In addition, any class that implements the interface can be passed as a procedure parameter that is declared as the interface's type. This allows for subclasses to be substituted for each other.

Sample Code

Here's an example that illustrates how to set up classes using `Implements` and how a client interacts with the classes. Suppose we have an abstract interface called `IabstractInterface` that has one method called `Execute`. The actual code for this class would be just the following procedure declaration:

```
Public Sub Execute()
End Sub
```

The procedure should not contain any code to implement the Execute method. Rather, concrete classes carry out the implementation. Each concrete class created should have `Implements IabstractInterface` in its Declarations section. This will add `IabstractInterface`'s `Execute` method to the concrete classes as a Private Sub. Since it is a Private Sub, clients cannot call directly to the concrete class. Rather, they have to call the interface class. So, let's say we had two concrete classes, cConcrete1 and cConcrete2. The code for the classes would be as follows:

```
'IabstractInterface
Public Sub Execute()
End Sub

'cConcrete1
Implements IabstractInterface
Private Sub IabstractInterface_Execute()
'implementation code for cConcrete1 goes here
End Sub
```

```
'cConcrete2
Implements IabstractInterface
Private Sub IabstractInterface_Execute()
'implementation code for cConcrete2 goes here
End Sub
```

A client form that wants to use a specific concrete class must first declare a variable of the abstract interface's type and then set it to reference an instance of the desired subclass. The client cannot call any of the interface's methods directly on the concrete class because those methods are Private within the concrete class. The client should call the interface. In turn, the interface will delegate the call to the concrete class that it was set to reference. Here's the code for the client:

```
Dim IobjInterface as IabstractInterface

Private Sub Form_Load()
set IobjInterface = New cConcrete1
End Sub


Private Sub Command1_Click()
IobjInterface.Execute
End Sub
```

Conclusion

Visual Basic object-based systems are aptly suited to take advantage of most design patterns. Design patterns provide flexibility by guiding the interaction between objects. Design patterns achieve this through decoupling objects, having the objects conform to a uniform interface, and by performing object substitution. Visual Basic's Implements keyword can be used to force compliance to a uniform interface and facilitate object substitution.

Structural Patterns

chapter 4

The Bridge Pattern

- Types of bridge patterns

- When to use a bridge pattern

- A UML diagram of a bridge pattern

- A sample use of a bridge pattern

- Other uses of a bridge

- Related patterns

A *bridge* pattern allows you to separate an interface from its implementation, so that the two can vary independently. This is just like a bridge in real life. It connects two, differing land masses. Similarly, a bridge pattern connects two, differing objects. The nice thing about software is that unlike real life, it's a lot easier to point the software bridge at a different object than it is to point a real bridge at a different land mass. Note that the word interface does not have anything to do with a Graphical User Interface (GUI). We are referring to the public properties and methods used to access the functionality that an object provides. The bridge pattern is most suited to situations where you want to build flexibility into the design of a system.

Types of Bridge Patterns

In a bridge pattern, a task is accomplished by two separate objects:

1. An *interface object*, which provides the public properties and methods for the calling program

2. An *implementation object*, which actually does the work.

The interface object calls the implementation object at run time. The calling program doesn't have to know about the implementation object. By varying the implementation objects, you can change the behavior without touching the calling code from the main program.

There are three main types of bridge implementations: *reference bridges*, *multiple bridges*, and *aggregation bridges*. The only difference between them is in how the interface object gets attached to and/or references the implementation object.

Reference Bridges

A reference bridge is implemented by giving the interface object a property that contains a reference to the implementation object. It allows you to vary the implementation at run time, but accesses only one implementation object at a time. Accessing the implementation is done through a line of code similar to this:

```
objImplementation.Execute()
```

Multiple Bridges

A multiple bridge is a reference bridge that uses a *member array* of implementation object references. (A member array is a property that is an array.) This allows the interface to call to multiple implementations, or to have a property or a mechanism to reckon the index of the implementation to use at the moment. In a multiple bridge, you would achieve the bridge as follows:

```
For Each Implementation In Implementations
    Implementation.Execute()
Next
```

Aggregation Bridges

An aggregation bridge is similar to a reference bridge except that the implementation object is a child of the interface object. In Visual Basic, you create this type of bridge through a collection. Calling the implementation would work exactly the same as a multiple bridge, and the code is identical:

```
For Each Implementation In Implementations
    Implementation.Execute()
Next
```

A UML Diagram of a Bridge Pattern

As shown in Figure 4.1, a bridge pattern simply delegates responsibility from one class to another. This allows you to vary the implementation at run time. In this approach, the client code calls the interface object's method, not knowing or caring that the implementation is actually being handled by another object. This allows you to standardize the calling of the method, while varying the code that runs by changing the implementation object.

Let's take a more detailed look at Figure 4.1, especially since it's the first example of a UML class diagram for a bridge (and, as we'll learn later, a bridge pattern forms a basis for many other patterns discussed in the book). In this diagram, we're highlighting only the main characteristics of the bridge. The AbstractInterface class is the one that you, as an application developer, will be working with. When the application calls the `Operation` method, it internally calls the Implementation classes' `OperationImplementation` method, as you can see from the note attached to the operation method. Although a particular instance of a bridge may use different names for the methods and classes, the idea is the same. The application calls a method of an object that provides an interface into a specific capability. That method delegates the responsibility for carrying out the capability to another object. That other object can be changed as often as necessary without affecting the core application.

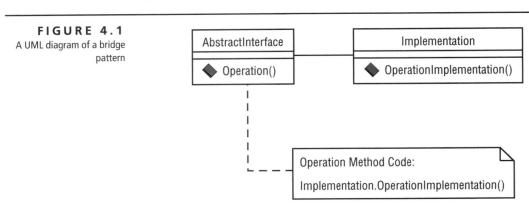

FIGURE 4.1
A UML diagram of a bridge pattern

A Sample Use of a Bridge Pattern

Let's take a look at an example of a bridge. Let's say we're building a system to track stock information as it comes in over an Internet connection. Our users need to be able to open multiple windows, and assign stocks to whichever windows they want. Each window displays stocks differently. For example, one type of window displays the stock and value in a grid. Another type displays only the stock identification in a form, and displays the value in a message box. Figure 4.2 shows a sample of the application at work.

FIGURE 4.2
Our sample application

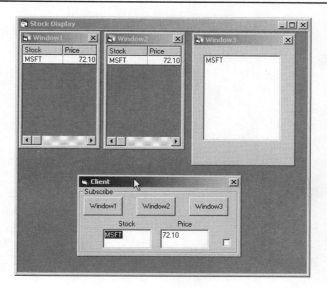

Applying the Bridge Pattern

As developers, we don't know which window type the user may select for any given stock. Nor do we know what new types of windows we may be asked to add to the system. As a result, it makes sense to decouple the information sent to your application (stock "x" now has a price of "y") from the action that results (display the values of the stock in the specified way for that particular window). So this is a perfect place for a bridge.

To create the bridge, we create two sets of classes: Subject and Publisher, allowing the former to handle capturing of the data, and using the latter to decide how to display the data. Our class design would look something like the one shown in Figure 4.3.

FIGURE 4.3
The subject and publisher
class diagram

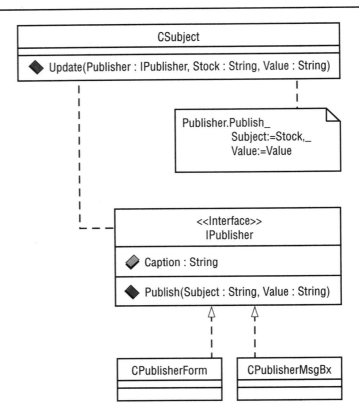

Both the hierarchy and the decoupling of the capture of information from the presentation of that information allows us great flexibility in our application design. The decoupling makes things flexible, while the hierarchy causes all of the objects that adhere to the implementation to implement the same classes, allowing the decoupling to take place easily. As you can see from the class diagram, the CSubject class provides the public interface for any stock-tracking client that we may create. The client simply calls the Update method. When a client asks the subject object to publish the information, the subject object passes the request to whichever publisher object it is currently connected with. The various publisher objects all implement the same IPublisher interface, ensuring that they have a Publish method that can be called. In this manner, we can use a grid or message box based form as the publishing mechanism. Adding a new type of publishing (maybe a graph) simply requires that we create a new class that implements the IPublisher interface, stores the values over time, and graphs them.

Calling the Bridge

Below is the important code that is used by our client (which is our main form) to set up and run the classes. As you read it, note that we instantiate the subject object and the interfaces for each publisher object in the declarations for the client. We then instantiate all the various forms for the publishers in the form load of our client, and set their captions so that we can easily refer to them. Finally, the command button's click selects one of the publisher interfaces, and passes it to the subject with the stock identification and price.

Note also that we create the publisher and subject objects separately. Then at the end, we simply tell the subject which publisher to use in displaying its information. This approach allows us to create an unlimited number of publisher classes, displaying stock information in as many ways as needed over the course of our application's lifetime.

```
'Declarations
Dim iobjStock1 As IPublisher
Dim iobjStock2 As IPublisher
Dim iobjStock3 As IPublisher
Dim objSubject As New cSubject

Private Sub Form_Load()
'Three windows are instantiated.
'In the Initialize event of each object the associated
'form is displayed.
'The interface object is set to its associated class.
'The interface methods must be called through the interface object,
    'although the class' method actually executes.
Set iobjStock3 = New cPublisherMsgbx
Set iobjStock2 = New cPublisherForm
Set iobjStock1 = New cPublisherForm
iobjStock1.Caption = "Window1"
iobjStock2.Caption = "Window2"
iobjStock3.Caption = "Window3"
End Sub

'Specific window is updated with stock info.
Private Sub cmdWindow_Click(Index As Integer)
Dim i As Integer
Dim bAdded As Boolean
Dim strStock As String
```

```
Dim strPrice As String
Dim obj As IPublisher
strStock = Trim(txtSubscribe.Text)
strPrice = Trim(txtPrice.Text)
If strStock = "" Or strPrice = "" Then Exit Sub
Select Case Index
Case 0
    Set obj = iobjStock1
Case 1
    Set obj = iobjStock2
Case 2
    Set obj = iobjStock3
End Select
objSubject.Update obj, strStock, strPrice
End Sub
```

Other Uses of a Bridge

The bridge is the most basic of flexibility patterns. Most of the patterns you will use—and most of the patterns discussed in this book—will be based on a bridge of some sort. Therefore, throughout the book we will use other pattern names to provide us with more specific details than the word bridge alone does. For instance, you can refer to something as a piece of furniture, something to sit on, or a wooden stool. All three are the same thing, but the third option is the most precise. Similarly, a design can be both a bridge and a *mediator*. The mediator pattern contains the bridge pattern within it—and uses the bridge to get things done—but a mediator is more complex than a bridge. Since mediator will more precisely describe what the purpose of the pattern is, we'll often use that term rather than the term bridge.

Other common uses of the bridge include:

- Decoupling status tracking from logging the status. In this case one object captures status information while the other is responsible for writing it to a table, event log, etcetera.

- Separating database functions from the execution of the function. In this case, one object provides the interface for database functionality (AddNew, Save, Delete) while the other object implements that functionality using ADO, DAO, RDO, native APIs, and so on.

- When a program accesses a database using ADO, it works with the ADO interface. ADO handles instantiating the correct database drivers and redirecting requests as necessary.

Related Patterns

The bridge pattern not only forms the basis of some patterns, like the mediator, but is also related to other patterns. For example, bridges are typically used when the flexibility is designed into the initial system. Adapter patterns, on the other hand, are usually used after a system is designed and you need to retrofit flexibility. Also related to the bridge, abstract factories are often used to create and configure bridges. The purpose of a factory is to standardize the creation of objects in a specific set of code, allowing the requirements for the objects to be set at run time. The requirements are often fulfilled through a bridge.

NOTE   Related to the bridge, adapter patterns are discussed in Chapter 5, "The Adapter Pattern," and abstract factories are discussed in Chapter 23, "The Factory Pattern."

Conclusion

The bridge pattern is most suited to situations where you want to build flexibility into the design of a system. It is used, among other things, to vary the implementation at run time. Think of this pattern when you want to define a fairly standard interface for an object, while changing the implementation of the object throughout the lifetime of the application. The bridge pattern also gives the application developer a smaller set of knowledge to deal with. The application developer only has to know about the interface object, and does not have to deal with implementation details.

chapter 5

The Adapter Pattern

- Two-way adapters

- A UML diagram of an adapter pattern

- A sample use of an adapter pattern

- Related patterns

An *adapter* allows a client object to call a server object even though the server object has an unrecognized or incompatible interface. An adapter is also known as a *wrapper* because the adapter object is like a communication layer that is wrapped around the server object. An adapter allows two incompatible objects to communicate by using an intermediary object that is compliant with both the client object and the server object. This intermediary object delegates the execution of the client requests to the incompatible server object.

For example, suppose that from within an *Active Server Page* (ASP) you want to use VBScript to call a non-COM *dynamic-link library* (DLL). Unfortunately, however, VBScript doesn't allow you to declare Windows API calls, because VBScript does not support the Declare statement used to declare API calls. So the non-COM DLL is incompatible with the ASP application. By using an adapter, you can work around this incompatibility by adapting the non-COM DLL to a COM interface, thereby enabling the client object and server object to communicate with each other.

Here's how you do it. You create a Visual Basic class module that has an identical public interface to the non-COM DLL. Internally this class module has the necessary API declarations and code to call the non-COM DLL. The VBScript in the ASP page calls the Visual Basic object, rather than the non-COM DLL. In turn, the VB object delegates the request to the non-COM DLL. This is how an adapter allows incompatible objects to interact with each other. Figure 5.1 depicts this process.

FIGURE 5.1
A sequence diagram that depicts how an adapter can be used to allow for VBScript to communicate with a Non-COM DLL

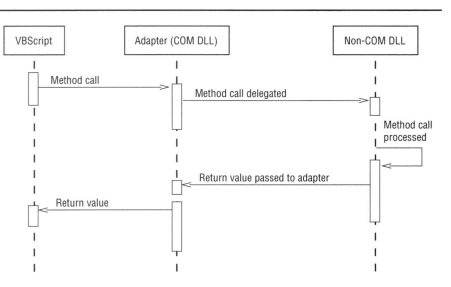

Sometimes, objects are incompatible because the client object expects a different interface than that provided by the server object. For example, let's say a client object calls methods or expects return values that aren't within the server object's public interface. In this case, an adapter class can be used as an intermediary object that receives the client's requests, translates them into a request that the server understands, and calls the server.

Two-way Adapters

Besides the simple adapter described above, there is another type of adapter called a *two-way adapter* . A two-way adapter is used when you want multiple objects to use an object, and each one of the objects expects a different interface. The two-way adapter works around this problem by having the adapter class implement multiple interfaces. As a result, the server object can communicate with multiple clients that call different interfaces. The section below, "A Sample Use of an Adapter," will explain how to implement a two-way adapter.

A UML Diagram of an Adapter Pattern

As you can see from the UML class diagram in Figure 5.2, an adapter is an intermediary object that facilitates the interaction between two otherwise incompatible objects.

FIGURE 5.2
A diagram of an adapter pattern

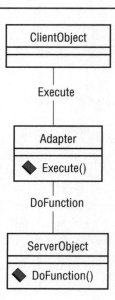

Figure 5.3 depicts a scenario where two clients are bound to two different interfaces. A two-way adapter that implements both interfaces is used to direct the clients' requests to a server object that fills the request.

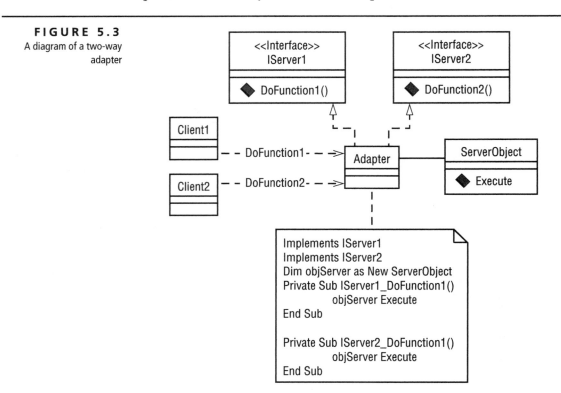

FIGURE 5.3
A diagram of a two-way adapter

A Sample Use of an Adapter Pattern

Suppose you are replacing the disk I/O routines of an existing software system. The existing system is composed of several components that use different utility objects for I/O. Let's say you would like to unify them to use one object for I/O, and you have chosen the relatively new FileSystemObject that is part of the Microsoft Scripting Runtime. There are three classes in the existing system, Status-Log, ErrorReporter, and UserOutput. Each one of these objects has a property called IOobject that points to an object that provides disk I/O services. However,

StatusLog, ErrorReporter, and UserOutput each expect a different object for the IOobject property. StatusLog uses FileLog, ErrorReport uses FileReport, and UserOutput uses FileOutput, as in Figure 5.4.

FIGURE 5.4
Software system in which
multiple objects are used
for disk I/O

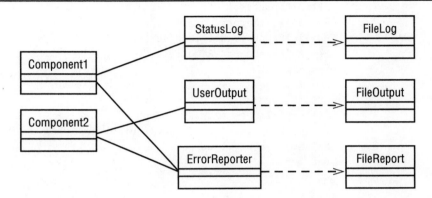

Although you have access to the Visual Basic project for the system, you cannot modify any of the existing classes to use the FileSystem object. With an adapter, however, you can have all of these components use the FileSystem object. Just create an adapter class that implements all of the individual I/O interfaces. This can be done using the Implements keyword. Once the adapter implements all the interfaces, it can be passed to any of the IOobject properties. The code would read as follows:

```
'FileLog class defines one public method:
Public Sub Save(Log as String)
End Sub

'FileReport class defines one public method:
Public Sub Write(Report as String)
End Sub

'FileOutput class defines one public method:
Public Sub SavetoFile(Value as String)
End Sub
```

StatusLog, ErrorReporter, and UserOutput classes have a property called IOobject that points to an object that provides disk I/O services:

```
'StatusLog:
Dim objFileLog as FileLog
```

```
Public Property Set_IOobject(Log as FileLog)
Set objFileLog=Log
End Sub

'ErrorReporter:
Dim objFileReport as Filereport
Public Property Set_IOobject(Report as FileReport)
Set objFileReport=Report
End Sub

'UserOutput:
Dim objFileOutput as FileOutput
Public Property Set_IOobject(Output as FileOutput)
Set objFileOutput=Output
End Sub
```

Here's how to use a two-way adapter to unify the objects to use the FileSystem-Object. Take a Visual Basic class module and write in the Declarations section:

```
Implements FileLog
Implements FileReport
Implements FileOutput
```

These statements will automatically import the procedure declarations of each interface into the adapter class:

```
Private Sub FileLog_Save(Log as String)
End Sub

Private Sub FileReport_Write(Report as String)
End Sub

Private Sub FileOutput_SavetoFile(Value as String)
End Sub
```

Note that the procedures are declared as *private*. Clients cannot access these procedures directly on the adapter class. They must first declare a variable of the interface's type and then set the variable to an instance of the adapter class.

In each one of the procedures, write code that uses the FileSystem object to write the information passed into the procedure to disk.

```
Implements FileLog
Implements FileReport
```

```
Implements FileOutput
Dim sFileName as String
Dim objFSO As New Scripting.FileSystemObject
Dim txt As Scripting.TextStream

Private Sub FileLog_Save(Log as String)
Set txt = objFSO.OpenTextFile(sFileName, ForWriting, True)
txt.Write Log
End Sub

Private Sub FileReport_Write(Report as String)
Set txt = objFSO.OpenTextFile(sFileName, ForWriting, True)
txt.Write Report
End Sub

Private Sub FileOutput_SavetoFile(Value as String)
Set txt = objFSO.OpenTextFile(sFileName, ForWriting, True)
txt.Write Value
End Sub
```

The client code that uses these objects would be as follows:

```
'Declare and instantiate components
Dim objStatusLog as StatusLog
Dim objErrorReporter as ErrorReporter
Dim objUserOutput as UserOutput

'declare interfaces do not instantiate
Dim objFileLog as FileLog
Dim objFileReport as FileReport
Dim objFileOutput as FileOutput

'instantiate adapter
Dim objAdapter as New Adapter

Private Sub Form_Load()
'set each interface variable to point to an instance of adapter
Set ObjFileLog = objAdapter
Set ObjFileReport = objAdapter
```

```
      Set ObjFileOutput = objAdapter
      'set the componenets' IOobject property to point to the expected
  'interface which actually contains an instance of adapter
      Set objStatusLog.IOobject= ObjFileLog
      Set objErrorReporter.IOobject = objFilereport
      Set objUserOutput.IOobject = objFileOutput
      End Sub
      'Declare and instantiate components
      Dim objStatusLog as StatusLog
      Dim objErrorReporter as ErrorReporter
      Dim objUserOutput as UserOutput

      'instantiate adapter
      Dim objAdapter as New Adapter

      Private Sub Form_Load()

      ObjAdapter.FileName = "C:\MyLogFile.log"
      'set the componenets'  IOobject property to point to the expected
  'interface which actually contains an 'instance of adapter
      Set objStatusLog.IOobject= objAdapter
      Set objErrorReporter.IOobject = objAdapter
      Set objUserOutput.IOobject = objAdapter
      End Sub
```

The client declares variables of each one of the I/O object types and then points them to an instance of the adapter class. Each one of the component's IOobjects is then set to its appropriate variable type. Each of these variables actually contains an instance of the adapter. When the components call the procedures of the I/O objects, the procedure calls are then delegated to the adapter class, and the adapter class executes the procedures using the FileSystem object. As you see from this example, an adapter can be used to wrap the FileSystem in an object that is compatible with varying clients. Figure 5.5 shows how the adapter implements all the old I/O object interfaces and redirects the client calls to the FileSystemObject.

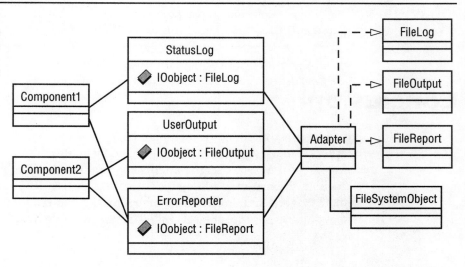

FIGURE 5.5
A diagram of the sample system after all the objects were unified to use the File-SystemObject for disk I/O

Related Patterns

The concept of an adapter is a basic design patterns concept and is used in several other patterns. For example, decorator, facade, and proxy also all use an interme-diate object between the client and server objects. An adapter is less complex than these other patterns, however. An adapter is simply used to allow commu-nication between incompatible objects. On the other hand, these other patterns aren't used to provide compatibility. Rather, they are used to enhance function-ality in some way.

Decorator is used to enhance the functionality of the object that is being deco-rated. It does so by inserting a decorator object between the client and server. The decorator delegates client calls to the server and also executes additional functionality.

Facade is used to simplify interaction between the client and a complex system of objects. It does so by inserting a facade object between the client and server. The facade object represents the underlying complex system of objects. Similarly, the proxy pattern uses an intermediary object as a surrogate object for the client to communicate with the server.

NOTE   For more information about these related patterns, see Chapter 7, "The Decorator Pattern" Chapter 8, "The Facade Pattern," and Chapter 10, "The Proxy Pattern."

Conclusion

An adapter is used to allow incompatible objects to interact. The concept behind adapters is to use an intermediary object to facilitate communication between two objects. This is a basic design patterns concept used in several other patterns. In particular, the two-way adapter illustrates the power of Visual Basic's `Implements` keyword. In this case, the `Implements` keyword allows an adapter object to masquerade as multiple objects by assuming multiple interfaces.

The Composite Pattern

- Types of composite patterns

- A UML diagram of a composite pattern

- A sample use of a composite pattern

- Sample code for a composite pattern

- Other uses of a composite

- Related patterns

The *composite* pattern provides a unified interface that both *collection classes* and *leaf node classes* can inherit. Collection classes are structures that contain references to other objects. Leaf node classes are singular objects that do not contain a collection of other objects. In a company's organizational chart, for example, you would have departments containing many employees. The departments are collections and the employees are leaf node classes. By defining one interface, clients can treat items and collections uniformly within a hierarchy. Client code can recursively iterate through a part-whole hierarchy without having to write separate code to distinguish between the collections and primitives. The composite pattern eliminates the need to write case statements that depend on the type of class when traversing a hierarchy.

The composite pattern can be used in many applications. Most graphical packages use a composite pattern to represent objects on the screen. Draw a few lines using Microsoft Word and then group them together. The set of lines now act as one object. This grouping represents a composite object containing several lines. Other uses of the composite pattern appear in every field. In the financial industry, portfolios are made of individual assets. Portfolios represent the composite and the assets are the individual objects contained in the portfolio. I am sure you can find many more examples in your own code where the composite pattern would be useful.

Types of Composite Patterns

The composite pattern can be structured in two different ways:

- The system is a strict hierarchy, where each child has one parent.

- An object is shared among multiple braches of a hierarchy and has multiple parents. This sharing of objects within the tree hierarchy is best handled using the flyweight.

NOTE   See Chapter 9, "The Flyweight Pattern," for more information.

In addition to these basic structures, there are several variations that can be made to these hierarchical composite pattern structures. These variations to both composite structures include:

- Varying the data structure for storing the child object

- Imposing an order on the objects within the hierarchy

- Allowing the child object to explicitly reference the parent objects

These variations on the composite pattern allow developers to customize the composite interface to the particular task. Let's look at each variation in more detail.

Modifying the storage structure for the child objects is a question of resources and performance. Different structures offer ease of development, like the dictionary or collection object, but incur a memory hit. A simple structure like an array would reduce the overhead associated with the collection object, but increase development complexity by forcing the developer to handle the resizing of the arrays when adding and removing objects.

Since certain applications require child objects to be in a specific order, whether it is simply an ordering of siblings within a family or a more complicated parsing tree, the interface to access the child objects needs to be designed to handle this ordering. The iterator pattern can help in traversing the composite objects, but the management of the individual objects will have to be designed carefully.

You can simplify the iteration through the composite structure by maintaining a circular reference between the parent and the child. That is to say, each parent maintains a reference to the child and each child maintains a reference to the parent. The traversal through the hierarchy is easier because the algorithm can backtrack up the hierarchy once it reaches a leaf node. The algorithm will not have to remember its path. If it reaches a dead end, it retrieves a reference to the parent object and continues on its way.

The easiest method to implement the circular reference between parent and child nodes is to manage the reference in the Add and Remove methods. When a child object is added to a collection, the child receives a reference to the collection. When it is removed from the collection, the reference is set to nothing. A simple example of this would be the following:

```
Implements IComposite
Dim oParent As IComposite
```

```
Private Property Set IComposite_Parent(oParent As IComposite)
    Set oParent = oParent
End Property

Private Sub IComposite_Add(oChild As IComposite)
    Set oChild.Parent = Me

    ' Code to add the child to the collection
End Sub

Private Sub IComposite_Remove(oChild As IComposite)
    Set oChild.Parent = Nothing

    ' Code to remove the child from the collection
End Sub
```

A UML Diagram of a Composite Pattern

At the heart of the composite pattern is the composite object. The composite object defines the interface used by both the collection and the singular object. Figure 6.1 displays a standard object model of the composite pattern.

The composite pattern consists of three main classes, IComposite, Composite, and Leaf. IComposite defines the interface for all of the objects. At a minimum, it must define operations for managing and accessing children within a collection. The basic methods for this are Add, Remove, and GetChild. In addition, the IComposite interface defines operations for the singular leaf objects of the hierarchy.

FIGURE 6.1
An object model of the
composite pattern

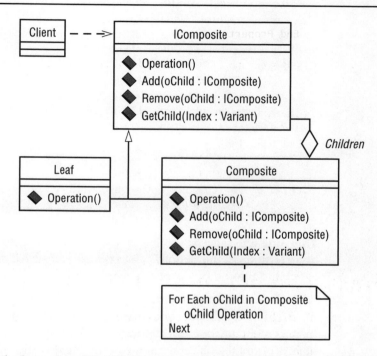

Creating the base class IComposite as an aggregate of the Leaf and Composite interfaces breaks slightly with good design practices for class hierarchies. Usually, you should only include operations in the base class that are used by all subclasses. In this pattern, however, the base class defines operations that are used mostly by the Composite object, but not by the Leaf object. The composite pattern is designed to provide transparency among the objects so clients do not have to treat a Leaf object differently from a Composite object. It is good programming practice to raise error 445 when you do not implement a method of an interface. If a client tries to access the Leaf's Add, Remove, or GetChild methods, then the methods should raise an error. The following shows these methods for the Leaf class:

```
Option Explicit
Implements IComposite
```

```
Private Const E_NOTIMPL = &H80004001

Private Sub IComposite_Add(oChild As IComposite)
    Err.Raise E_NOTIMPL, "Leaf.Add"
End Sub

Private Function IComposite_GetChild(Index As Variant) As _
 IComposite
    Err.Raise E_NOTIMPL, "Leaf.GetChild"
End Function


Private Sub IComposite_Remove(oChild As IComposite)
    Err.Raise E_NOTIMPL, "Leaf.Remove"
End Sub
```

This code will raise an error with the standard Windows error message "Object doesn't support this action." This code will ensure that the contract between the client and the composite object is upheld.

The Leaf class implements the behavior of primitive singular objects within the hierarchy. They do not contain any children. The Composite class implements the management functions for children and also implements the operations of the child objects. From the object model, you can see that the Operation method will iterate through all of the child objects and call the Operation method on the children. This process allows operations to be propagated throughout the entire hierarchy without having to traverse the entire tree.

Lastly, adding other operations to the IComposite interface can extend the pattern. As discussed above, the IComposite interface can allow clients to retrieve a reference to the parent object in the hierarchy. Adding a GetParent method to the IComposite interface would allow clients to retrieve the parent object.

A Sample Use of a Composite Pattern

The composite pattern can be used to represent any *part-whole hierarchy*. A part-whole hierarchy, or *part-whole relationship*, arises from a relationship of containership. That is to say, one object is completely contained within another. In addition, a part-whole hierarchy represents an aggregate object that is physically made of other objects (like a book, which is an aggregate of pages).

There are many instances where you will want to implement part-whole hierarchies within an application. For example:

- Family trees

- Some graphics systems, especially ones that:

  - Group objects together

  - Form compound objects from primitive objects like lines and arcs

- Any type of equipment, including:

  - Cars

  - Computers

Assume that you are building an application for a car manufacturer. The application will be used to assemble the different pieces of a car and calculate the total cost of the car based on the cost of each piece. This application will need to catalog all of the parts within a car. The composite pattern comes into play because assembling the different pieces of the car together represents a composite, or part-whole hierarchy. The car is the whole, aggregate object; and each part—the door, wheel, engine—represent individual objects within the car. Figure 6.2 depicts a simple class structure that can be used in the application.

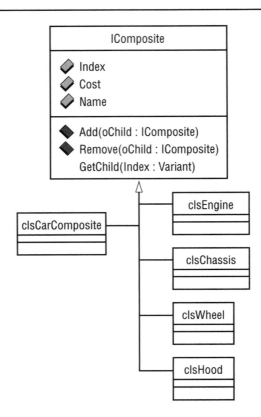

FIGURE 6.2
An object model of a
sample car application

Sample Code for a Composite Pattern

This car manufacturing application consists of one abstract interface, IComposite, along with two collections, clsCarComposite and clsChassis, and three primitive leaf classes, clsEngine, clsHood, and clsWheel. Obviously this is not an exhaustive list of components in a car, just a starting point. The application allows you to assemble different cars and compute the price of the final assembly. The interface to which all of the composite objects conform is defined in IComposite as follows:

```
' IComposite Interface
Public Property Get Index() As Variant
End Property
```

```
Public Property Let Index(Value As Variant)
End Property

Public Property Get Name() As String
End Property

Public Property Let Name(Value As String)
End Property

Public Property Get Cost() As Single
End Property

Public Sub add(oChild As IComposite)
End Sub

Public Sub Remove(oChild As IComposite)
End Sub

Public Function GetChild(Index As Variant) As IComposite
End Function
```

IComposite defines three methods and three properties. The three methods are only used within the composite classes, the properties are used by all subclasses.

The two composite classes have similar code behind them. The difference between the two would be that the car may have other properties associated with it, like VIN. As a result of the similar implementation, the following code is representative of the aggregate functionality within the clsCarComposite and clsChassis classes:

```
Implements IComposite

Private oCollection As New Collection
Private vIndex As Variant
Private sName As String

Private Sub IComposite_add(oChild As IComposite)
    oCollection.add oChild, oChild.Index
End Sub
```

```
Private Property Get IComposite_Cost() As Single
    Dim sngCost As Single
    Dim oChild As IComposite

    For Each oChild In oCollection
        sngCost = sngCost + oChild.Cost
    Next

    IComposite_Cost = sngCost
End Property

Private Function IComposite_GetChild(Index As Variant) _
As IComposite
    Set IComposite_GetChild = oCollection.Item(Index)
End Function

Private Property Let IComposite_Index(RHS As Variant)
    vIndex = RHS
End Property

Private Property Get IComposite_Index() As Variant
    IComposite_Index = vIndex
End Property

Private Property Let IComposite_Name(RHS As String)
    sName = RHS
End Property

Private Property Get IComposite_Name() As String
    IComposite_Name = sName
End Property

Private Sub IComposite_Remove(oChild As IComposite)
    oCollection.Remove oChild.Index
End Sub
```

The composite classes store the children within a collection object, oCollection. The Add, Remove, and GetChild methods just wrap the functionality of the Add, Remove, and Item methods of the collection object. The cost property iterates through the child objects in order to calculate the price. The rest of the methods are just to set or retrieve the properties of the object.

The leaf objects also share a similar implementation, so the following code represents the code behind the clsHood, clsWheel, and clsEngine classes:

```
Implements IComposite

Private vIndex As Variant
Private sName As String
Private sngCost As Single

Private Sub Class_Initialize()
    sngCost = 1983.56
End Sub

Private Sub IComposite_add(oChild As IComposite)
    Err.Raise E_NOTIMPL, "clsEngine.Add"
End Sub

Private Property Get IComposite_Cost() As Single
    IComposite_Cost = sngCost
End Property

Private Function IComposite_GetChild(Index As Variant) _
 As IComposite
    Err.Raise E_NOTIMPL, "clsEngine.GetChild"
End Function

Private Property Let IComposite_Index(RHS As Variant)
    vIndex = RHS
End Property

Private Property Get IComposite_Index() As Variant
    IComposite_Index = vIndex
End Property

Private Property Let IComposite_Name(RHS As String)
    sName = RHS
End Property

Private Property Get IComposite_Name() As String
    IComposite_Name = sName
End Property
```

```
Private Sub IComposite_Remove(oChild As IComposite)
    Err.Raise E_NOTIMPL, "clsEngine.Remove"
End Sub
```

Here you can see that the management functions that handle child objects raise an error message if they are called. This ensures that the contract between the client and the object is maintained. You could leave these procedures as empty procedures such as:

```
Private Sub IComposite_Add(oChild As IComposite)
End Sub
```

But this leads the client to believe that the object contains children and in reality this information has been lost. The leaf did not store a reference to the child and the client could have erased the reference when it tried to add it. This puts the class hierarchy into a state that the client was not expecting. In general, if a method is not implemented within a subclass, the method should raise an error.

Lastly, the client code to create the composite and to calculate the price is behind the form. The following code builds the composite hierarchy:

```
Private Enum CarPart
    cpCarComposite
    cpChassis
    cpEngine
    cpFrame
    cpHood
    cpWheel
End Enum

Private Sub BuildCar()
    Dim oCar As IComposite
    Dim oChassis As IComposite

    Set oCar = MakePart(cpCarComposite, "Jaguar XK120", _
        "JXK120")
    Set oChassis = MakePart(cpChassis, "Jaguar XK120 Chassis", _
        "CH1")

    oChassis.add MakePart(cpHood, "Hood", "HD1")
```

```
        oCar.add oChassis
        oCar.add MakePart(cpEngine, "Jaguar Inline 6 cylinder", _
          "EG1")
        oCar.add MakePart(cpWheel, "Front Left Wire Wheel", "FLW")
        oCar.add MakePart(cpWheel, "Front Right Wire Wheel", "FRW")
        oCar.add MakePart(cpWheel, "Rear Left Wire Wheel", "RLW")
        oCar.add MakePart(cpWheel, "Rear Right Wire Wheel", "RRW")

         MsgBox oCar.Cost

    End Sub

    Private Function MakePart(pType As CarPart, pName As String, _
        pIndex As Variant) As IComposite
        Dim oPart As IComposite
        Select Case pType
            Case cpCarComposite
                Set oPart = New clsCarComposite
            Case cpChassis
                Set oPart = New clsChassis
            Case cpEngine
                Set oPart = New clsEngine
            Case cpHood
                Set oPart = New clsHood
            Case cpWheel
                Set oPart = New clsWheel
        End Select

        oPart.Name = pName
        oPart.Index = pIndex

        Set MakePart = oPart
    End Function
```

The BuildCar method simply instantiates each part using the MakePart method
and then assigns the object to one of the collections using the Add method of the
collection.

Lastly, the price is calculated by retrieving the Cost of the oCar object, which in turn iterates through each of its children to calculate the price. The call is simply:

```
MsgBox oCar.Cost
```

This sample application can be expanded in many ways. Since the implementation of most of the objects is similar, the application can share resources by implementing the hierarchy using the flyweight pattern. In addition, an iterator pattern can be used to traverse the hierarchy and calculate the price of the car.

Other Uses of a Composite

The composite pattern is useful when trying to create any part-whole hierarchy. It simplifies the interface for interacting with the hierarchy by combining the composite methods with the leaf methods. The sample application above implemented one common part-whole hierarchy, but many applications model a similar situation. The composite pattern can be used in a reporting application to represent the different bands within the report. It can be used in graphics programs to model the group of elementary objects into complex structures like those drawn in CAD programs. One very useful application within VB is to represent the hierarchy displayed in a tree view control. Each node of the tree view could map to an object within the composite hierarchy.

Related Patterns

The composite pattern can be used in conjunction with the iterator pattern and the flyweight pattern. You can use the iterator pattern to traverse the hierarchy defined in the composite pattern. In addition, you can use the iterator to find a specific node in the hierarchy or to aggregate certain properties of the hierarchy. In the sample application above, an iterator could be used to calculate the price.

The flyweight is useful for sharing resources among a few objects. It alleviates the need to instantiate objects for each node within the hierarchy. The hierarchy then becomes a web where one leaf appears in multiple branches of the hierarchy.

> **NOTE** Related to the composite, you can learn more about the iterator pattern in Chapter 16 and the flyweight pattern in Chapter 9.

Conclusion

The composite pattern offers a nice method of simplifying interactions between a client and a hierarchical tree structure. It allows the client to interact with only one class and does not have to make a distinction between a collection class and a leaf class. It does this by defining one interface that is an aggregate of the collection interface and the leaf interface.

chapter 7

The Decorator Pattern

- When to use a decorator pattern

- A UML diagram of a decorator pattern

- A sample decorator pattern

- Related patterns

The *decorator* pattern is an alternative to implementation inheritance. Since VB does not currently support implementation inheritance, the decorator pattern has proven extremely valuable to VB developers. In addition, the decorator pattern is even more flexible than inheritance. With implementation inheritance, if functionality were added to a class, then all of its subclasses would inherit that functionality. This creates an inflexible hierarchy that is not applicable in all circumstances. In contrast, the decorator pattern allows additional responsibilities to be assigned to an object without subclassing. The decorator provides an alternative to implementation inheritance by allowing a decorator object to add functionality dynamically to another object. Significantly, it does so without modifying the interface of the original object. Another benefit of the decorator pattern is that functionality can be added or removed from the object without modifying the decorated object's code.

The decorator pattern works by enclosing an object within a decorator object. The decorator object then adds functionality. Since the interface is not modified—and must be implemented completely by the decorator object—multiple decorators can be stacked in order to provide layers of functionality that are added dynamically to an object. Best of all, the decorator pattern provides this additional functionality without either modifying the original object or creating an inflexible class hierarchy through implementation inheritance.

The basic idea of a decorator involves creating a class that has a method for every function or method used in the object you are decorating. Within these method calls, additional functionality can be added and then a call to the original object's method is made. If the decorator object does not implement a method of the interface, then the decorator must pass control through to the decorated object.

When to Use a Decorator Pattern

You can use the decorator pattern whenever you need to add functionality to an object. Perhaps you want to separate out a function from an object you just created to provide cleaner, more flexible code. Or perhaps you do not have access to the original source code from a third-party product. Often third-party products implement most of the functionality that you require, but there is almost always something missing. When something is missing, you can wrap the third-party objects in a decorator object to provide the missing functionality. This allows you to extend the objects without changing the interface or code of the original objects.

It is often useful to extend the third-party product ActiveX Data Objects (ADO). ADO performs most of the functionality required in a typical database application. Even so, sometimes you need to extend the functionality of ADO. As an example, let's extend the ADO save method on the recordset by adding a logging feature that writes to the event log. You would implement the following save method in the decorator class:

```
' LogADOUpdate class
Public Sub Save()
    ' Call the decorated object's save method
    objDecorated.save

    ' Implement the additional functionality
    App.LogEvent "ADO Recordset updated", _
        VbLogEventTypeInformation
End Sub
```

Notice, no modifications were made to the original decorated class. Only new functionality was added to the class by adding a level of indirection between the client object and the object being decorated. This type of indirection could be performed many times. Another decorator object could be used to validate the recordset before it was saved. So the validating class's save method would look like the following:

```
' ValidateADOUpdate class
Public Sub Save()
    ' Validate that the first name and last name
    ' are not blank
    If rs("FirstName") = "" Or rs("LastName") = "" Then

        Err.Raise vbObjectError + 514, _
            "ValidateADRS.Save", _
            "First and last name cannot be blank"
        Exit Sub
    End If

    ' Call the LogADOUpdate's save method
    oDecorated.Save
End Sub
```

As you can see in the two examples, the decorated code can act as pre- and post-conditions to the original code. The decorated code for the logging class happens after the save method is called, whereas the validation code is executed prior to executing the decorated save method.

A UML Diagram of a Decorator Pattern

The decorator pattern consists of four different classes, as shown in Figure 7.1. The figure shows a *base class component* that defines the interface for all of the other classes in the diagram. In this diagram, the ConcreteComponent is the original class. We will extend the ConcreteComponent with the decorators (ConcreteDecoratorA and ConcreteDecoratorB). In other words, the decorator objects will add to the ConcreteComponent any new functionality—or new responsibilities—that the application requires.

Since VB does not support multiple levels of inheritance, the decorator pattern cannot be implemented in the same manner as described in the GOF book. Instead, the concrete decorator classes will inherit the interface of the component class. The concrete decorator classes also maintain a reference to the component class being decorated.

FIGURE 7.1
A class diagram for the decorator pattern

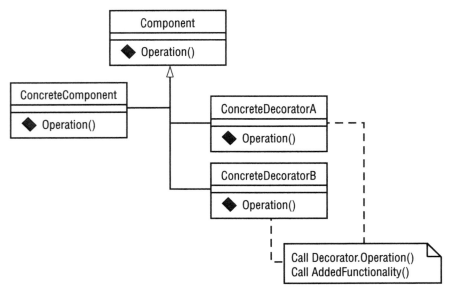

Figure 7.2 shows the sequence of events that occurs at run time when the decorator is called. The diagram depicts the cascading effect that occurs within the decorator. The decorator performs some specific functionality and then cascades the event down to other decorators or to the original component object. In this example, two decorators adorn the component object.

FIGURE 7.2
A sequence diagram of events depicts calling an operation of a decorator

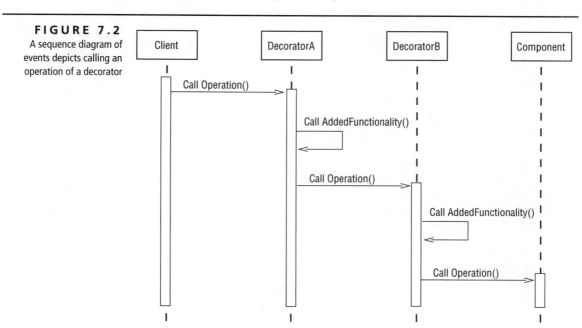

A Sample Decorator Pattern

This example shows how a charting application changes the appearance of a chart by using a decorator pattern. Figure 7.3 shows the line chart form with all of the decorators in use.

FIGURE 7.3
A charting application
implemented with a
decorator pattern

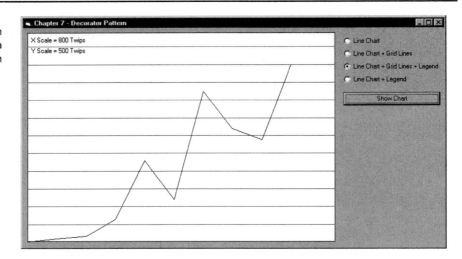

The application is composed of two decorator classes (LegendLineChart and
GridLineChart) and an original class (LineChart), as shown in the class diagram in
Figure 7.4.

FIGURE 7.4
A class diagram of a
charting application

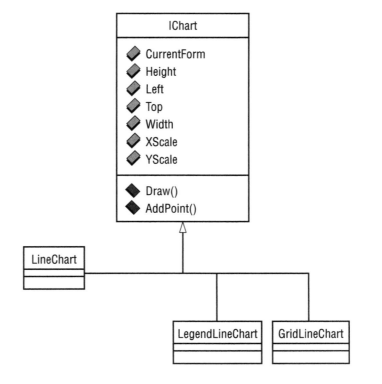

Both LegendLineChart and GridLineChart are implemented as decorators to the LineChart class. The code to call the different classes and to decorate the line chart is contained in the click method, as shown in the code below:

```
Private Sub cmdShowChart_Click()
    Dim DecoratorA As GridLineChart
    Dim DecoratorB As LegendLineChart
    Dim Component As LineChart

    Dim oChart As IChart
    Dim i As Integer

    Me.Cls

    ' Display the line chart
    If optGraph(0).value = True Then
        Set oChart = New LineChart
    End If

    ' Display the line chart with grid lines
    If optGraph(1).value = True Then
        Set DecoratorA = New GridLineChart
        DecoratorA.init New LineChart

        Set oChart = DecoratorA
    End If

    ' Display Line chart with grid lines and legend
    If optGraph(2).value = True Then
        Set DecoratorA = New GridLineChart
        Set DecoratorB = New LegendLineChart

        DecoratorB.init New LineChart

        DecoratorA.init DecoratorB

        Set oChart = DecoratorA
    End If

    ' Display line chart with legend
    If optGraph(3).value = True Then
        Set DecoratorB = New LegendLineChart
        DecoratorB.init New LineChart
```

```
        Set oChart = DecoratorB
    End If

    ' Set the variables for the chart and draw the chart
    oChart.Left = Shape1.Left
    oChart.Top = Shape1.Top
    oChart.Width = Shape1.Width
    oChart.Height = Shape1.Height

    oChart.XScale = 800
    oChart.YScale = 500
    Set oChart.CurrentForm = Me

    For i = 1 To 10
        oChart.AddPoint arrPoints(i)

    Next

    oChart.Draw
End Sub
```

This code sets up the classes so that they call each other in a hierarchy. The hierarchy of objects is depicted in Figure 7.5. The hierarchy is built by passing an IChart object into the *init* method of the decorator objects.

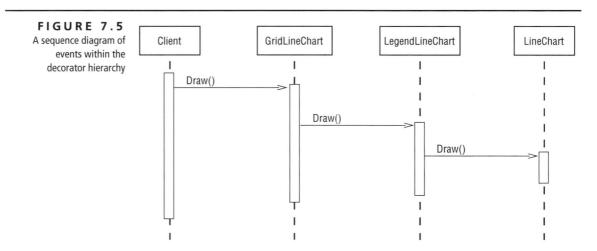

FIGURE 7.5
A sequence diagram of events within the decorator hierarchy

Each individual method call to GridLineChart is passed along to the object lower in the hierarchy. The main method within the sample is the Draw method. The Draw method for the LineChart class is shown below:

```
Private Sub IChart_Draw()
    Dim i As Integer
    Dim x1 As Double
    Dim y1 As Double
    Dim x2 As Double
    Dim y2 As Double

    frmCurrentForm.ForeColor = &HFF0000

    For i = 1 To UBound(arrPoints) - 1
        x1 = (arrPoints(i).x * lXScale) + lLeft
        x2 = (arrPoints(i + 1).x * lXScale) + lLeft
        y1 = lTop + lHeight - (arrPoints(i).y * lYScale)
        y2 = lTop + lHeight - (arrPoints(i + 1).y * _
            lYScale)

        frmCurrentForm.Line (x1, y1)-(x2, y2)
    Next

    frmCurrentForm.ForeColor = &H0
End Sub
```

The code simply iterates through the points and draws a line on the form. Since this method is implemented in the concrete component, it does not need to forward any method calls to the other objects. On the other hand, GridLineChart is a decorator in the sample application, so it needs to forward method calls to the object it is decorating. This is shown in the code below:

```
Private Sub IChart_Draw()
    Dim i As Integer
    Dim x1 As Long
    Dim x2 As Long
    Dim y As Long

    x1 = lLeft
    x2 = lLeft + lWidth

    frmCurrentForm.ForeColor = &H808080
```

```
' Draw grid lines
For i = 1 To 11
    y = lTop + lHeight - (i * lYScale)
    frmCurrentForm.Line (x1, y)-(x2, y)
Next

frmCurrentForm.ForeColor = &H0

oComponent.Draw
End Sub
```

Here the method is forwarded by the call to oComponent.Draw. oComponent can be either another decorator or the concrete component.

Related Patterns

A number of patterns are related to the decorator pattern. As discussed in this chapter, the decorator pattern adds new responsibilities to the object, but it does not change the object's interface. The adapter pattern, on the other hand, does change an object's interface. For this reason, the adapter pattern is often used to standardize an object's interface.

The decorator pattern's intent, moreover, is to add functionality to an object. In so doing, it creates an aggregate object similar to that created with the composite pattern.

Finally, the decorator pattern allows an object to change by building a hierarchy of objects, where each object adds a new responsibility. In contrast, the strategy pattern allows an algorithm to vary by encapsulating the algorithm within an object that conforms to a standard interface. This allows the algorithms to be changed dynamically.

NOTE   Read more about related patterns in Chapter 5, "The Adapter Pattern," Chapter 6, "The Composite Pattern," and Chapter 22, "The Strategy Pattern."

Conclusion

The decorator pattern is a powerful tool for VB developers because it offers an alternative to implementation inheritance. It allows developers to add new functionality or responsibilities to an object without modifying the original object's implementation. The decorator pattern provides a flexible means to combine objects at run time in order to modify an object. In the charting application, for example, we were able to create four different objects by dynamically combining three objects. If we had made this application using implementation inheritance, we would have had to create one base class and three subclasses.

chapter 8

The Facade Pattern

- A UML diagram of a facade pattern

- A sample use of a facade pattern

- Related patterns

The *facade* pattern provides a relatively simple interface to a complex subsystem or set of subsystems. Many systems provide their services through multiple subsystems or through calling multiple procedures. In order for clients to use the services of these systems, they would have to be familiar with the intricacies of its subsystems and procedures. Facade shields clients from the intricacies of the subsystems by providing a simple interface for clients to call. The facade in turn makes the necessary calls to its constituents to provide the service.

Facade is a common and useful pattern. In fact, all Visual Basic developers use the facade pattern every day. Visual Basic itself is a facade to the Windows operating system. When Visual Basic developers create forms, controls, menus, or raise and catch events, they do not need to know which API kernel to call or how to convert Visual Basic data types to C data types. All they need to know is how to use the relatively simple Visual Basic environment that acts as a facade to the Windows API.

A facade should shield clients from the intricacies of a system, but should not make the subsystems inaccessible. After all, a client might need a service of a subsystem to which the facade does not provide access. For example, as a facade, Visual Basic allows developers to directly call the Windows API to perform functions that Visual Basic itself does not surface up.

A UML Diagram of a Facade Pattern

As you can see from Figure 8.1, the facade provides a simple unified interface to a complex set of objects. A client object does not need to know anything about the subsystems to use the facade. Facade provides the interface for the client and delegates the tasks to its subsystems.

FIGURE 8.1
A UML diagram of a facade
pattern

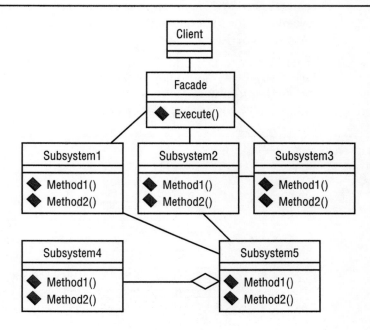

A Sample Use of a Facade Pattern

Suppose you are writing a medical search engine. The search engine searches based on the name of a medical condition and returns a list of doctors, medications, and articles associated with the condition. The search engine searches several databases of varying format and it also searches the Internet. This search engine will be sold to medical facilities to integrate into their existing software solutions. Each type of search has its own class, so we have four classes. A DoctorSearch class, a MedicationSearch class, an ArticleSearch class, and an InternetSearch class. Some of the classes require processing of the search criteria before they can perform the search.

For example, DoctorSearch only accepts medical specialties so the medical condition criteria must be linked to a specialty. ArticleSearch will provide better results if it searches based on both a medical condition and any drugs that treat the condition, so MedicationSearch should be run before ArticleSearch. Our sample facade will shield client applications from the intricacies of executing all the searches. In addition, rather than providing separate lists from each search, it will consolidate the material and return only one list of results from all of the searches the system performs.

For this scenario, we'll implement a facade pattern that provides a client interface with one method called Search. This method will call each one of the search objects and its prerequisites, and then compile all the results into one recordset. Figure 8.2 shows the object model for this application.

FIGURE 8.2

An object model of a search engine using the facade pattern

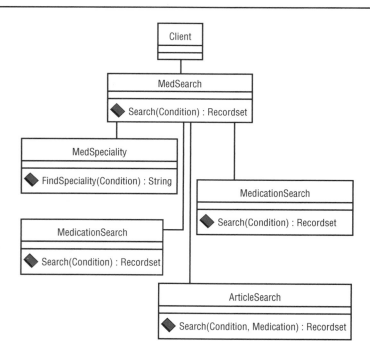

In this sample, the MedSearch object is the facade and the individual Search objects are the subsystems. The client application only has to call MedSearch's Search method and receives back one recordset with all the results. MedSearch executes all the individual searches and combines them all into one recordset and returns it to the client. Here's the code for the MedSearch's Search method:

```
Public Function Search(Condition as String)As ADODB.Recordset
Dim rsDoc as ADODB.recordset
Dim rsDrug as ADODB.recordset
Dim rsArticle as ADODB.recordset
Dim rsInternet as ADODB.recordset
```

```
Dim rsResults as New ADODB.Recordset
Dim objDoc as New DoctorSearch
Dim objDrug as New MedicationSearch
Dim objInternet as New InternetSearch
Dim objArticle as New ArticleSearch
Dim objSpecialty as New MedSpecialty
Dim strSpecialty as String
Dim strDrugs as String
'************Execute the Searches***************'
'********Get Medical specialty for Condition
strSpecialty=objSpecialty.FindSpecialty(Condition)
'*********Get list of doctors based on thear speciality
Set rsDoc=objDoc.Search(strSpecialty)
'*********Get a list of doctors based on condition
Set rsDrug=objDrug.Search(Condition)
'*********Get list of drugs in the form of a delimited string to pass
as a parameter to ArticleSearch
strDrugs=rsDrugs.GetString
Set rsArticle=objArticle.Search(Condition,strDrugs)
'********Search the internet for doctors based on condition
Set rsInternet = objInternet.Search(Condition)
'*********Create a recordset to contain all the results
With rsResults.Fields
.Append cType, adBSTR
.Append cValue, adBSTR
End With
rsResults.Open
'
'code that loops through each
'recordset and adds it to rsResults
'
Set Search=rsResults
End Function
```

Related Patterns

The facade pattern is similar to other patterns, including the mediator and decorator patterns, in terms of the way they act for other objects. Facade differs from decorator in that facade does not provide any new functionality. Rather, it abstracts existing functionality into an easy-to-use interface for clients. Decorator, on the other hand, is inserted between the client and server objects in order to enhance the server object.

The mediator pattern is used for regulating communication between colleague objects and is therefore bidirectional, while facade is used to simplify the client's access to the server objects, and is therefore unidirectional.

NOTE   Read more about the decorater pattern in Chapter 7 and the mediator patttern in Chapter 12.

Conclusion

The facade pattern is best suited for when a server system provides a service that is made up of multiple small services provided by individual subsystems. When a client doesn't need to access the subsystems for their individual services, facade provides an interface that gives a client one simple point of access to the composite service—without having to get down to the granular level of the subsystem.

The downside to the facade pattern is that the facade may obscure some functionality of the subsystems. As a result, when the need arises, the use of the facade pattern may require client applications to dig into little known API's to achieve a desired functionality.

chapter 9

The Flyweight Pattern

- When to use a flyweight pattern

- A UML diagram for a flyweight pattern

- A sample flyweight pattern

- Related patterns

The *flyweight* pattern provides a method to pool and share a large number of contexts. It allows a single object to be used in several contexts simultaneously. This pattern allows developers to design applications from an object-orientated view without the cost of instantiating a large number of objects, which could be prohibitive and inefficient.

At the heart of the flyweight pattern is the flyweight object. The flyweight object is shared among multiple contexts. This means that the flyweight object can exist in an application as a single instance, but, under different conditions, can represent different objects.

The flyweight achieves this reuse of objects at run time by dividing the state of an object into two categories, *intrinsic state* and *extrinsic state*. Intrinsic state is any state that can be shared across multiple contexts. It makes no assumptions about the current context of the object. Extrinsic state is a context-specific state. It is a state that cannot be shared across multiple contexts. When methods of the flyweight object are called, the extrinsic state must be passed to the methods from the client objects. This means that the client objects must store the extrinsic state of the flyweight object.

When to Use a Flyweight Pattern

The flyweight pattern is used only in certain situations. The application must meet two criteria, or else the flyweight pattern will not be effective. First, to warrant the use of the flyweight pattern, the application must use a large number of objects. Granted, large is a vague term to use for this criterion, but the exact number of objects will depend on several factors. The most significant determining factor is that instantiating all of the objects produces an inefficient application. The use of the flyweight pattern reduces the number of objects used, and thus increases the efficiency of the application.

Second, to use the flyweight pattern, the state of most of the objects must be made extrinsic. To make the state of the objects extrinsic, you can remove and store the extrinsic aspects in the client objects that call the flyweight. The idea is that the removal and storage of an extrinsic state in some other structure reduces the total amount of storage or memory used within your application. It would not be useful to create as many different kinds of external states as there are objects that were used in the first place. The external structure that stores this state can be as simple as an array or as complicated as another class.

Once you have removed the extrinsic state from the objects, you then need to determine whether relatively few shared objects can replace the remaining objects. An example of a drawing application will illustrate what this means. For simplicity, the drawing application only draws rectangles and the user can draw thousands of rectangles on the screen at a time. If a new object were instantiated for each rectangle that was drawn, there would be thousands of objects in memory at any time. This could lead to a performance problem. The external state of the rectangle would be the position of the rectangle, its top, left, height, and width properties. This extrinsic state could be stored in an array and passed into just one instantiated rectangle object, whenever the rectangle was moved and changed. By removing the extrinsic state, the application only has to instantiate one object instead of thousands. This is what it means to replace the remaining objects with relatively few objects once the extrinsic state has been removed.

The immediate advantage for your application is the reduction of objects in memory, which could improve the performance of the application. The one downside to consider is the performance hit in trying to associate an extrinsic state with an object. Since the state has been disassociated from the object, a method to associate the state with the object needs to be implemented, which could affect performance.

Using a Flyweight Pattern with a Document Editor

The best way to think about the flyweight is to consider a document editor application. If the application were to instantiate an object for each character in the document, the number of objects would eventually bring a computer to a crawl. If, however, the application created a pool of character objects representing the different letters in the alphabet—and only instantiated those character objects—there would be a total of approximately 100 objects, 52 letter objects (both upper and lower case), 10 digits, and the other keys. This reduces the number of objects from hundreds of thousands to one hundred.

To drastically reduce the total number of objects, certain aspects of the character objects must be made extrinsic. Two aspects that must be made extrinsic, for example, are the formatting and positioning of the characters.. By moving these aspects of the character's state out of the object, the flyweight must receive this information through its methods. To draw a character, the draw method needs to receive information about the character's intended position and font. This allows the character object to be used throughout the application. At the same time, it allows the font and position to change on the fly, since these aspects are external to the character.

A UML Diagram for a Flyweight Pattern

The flyweight pattern is composed of three main objects, the FlyweightFactory, the Flyweight, and the ConcreteFlyweight, as shown in Figure 9.1.

FIGURE 9.1
An object model of a
generic flyweight

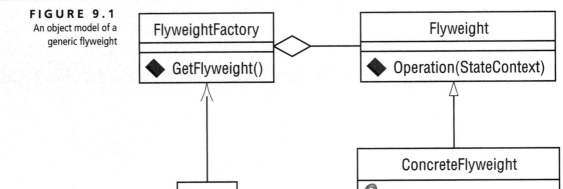

The flyweight object defines the interface that all of the concrete flyweights will implement. The flyweight object defines how the extrinsic state is passed to the ConcreteFlyweight objects. The ConcreteFlyweight is a subclass of the flyweight object. It adds a private memory variable for the intrinsic state. The intrinsic state stored by the ConcreteFlyweight must be sharable across multiple contexts.

The FlyweightFactory provides a method to create and manage the pool of flyweight objects. The FlyweightFactory returns a reference to an existing object if one exists in the pool of flyweight objects. If one does not exist in the pool, it instantiates a new object and returns a reference to that one.

The client object stores the extrinsic state of the flyweight objects. It passes this extrinsic state into the flyweight whenever a call is made to a method of the flyweight object.

A Sample Flyweight Pattern

A good example of the use of the flyweight pattern is the video game Asteroids, as shown in Figure 9.2.

FIGURE 9.2
The game Asteroids is implemented using a fly-weight pattern

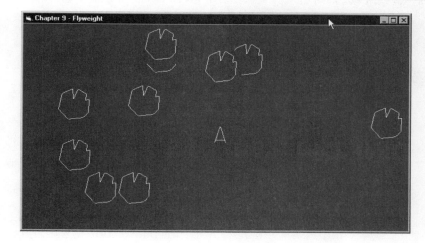

In many video games, a lot of objects perform many different actions at once. The state of these objects can be divided into extrinsic and intrinsic states. In Asteroids, the size and shape of the rocks is made intrinsic. There are only three different sized rocks, so there will only have to be three instantiated flyweight objects to handle all of the rocks. The speed, location, and direction of the rocks is made extrinsic to the flyweight object. By moving these context-specific states out of the flyweight, the application is able to handle a large number of contexts with only three instantiated objects.

The interface of the flyweight objects is defined in IAsteroidFlyweight:

```
'IAsteroidFlyweight
Enum astState
    LargeRock
    MediumRock
    SmallRock
End Enum

Public Property Let State(Value As astState)

End Property
```

```
Public Sub Initialize(oForm As Form, Index As Integer, _
    x As Long, y As Long)

End Sub

Public Sub Destroy(oForm As Form, Index As Integer)

End Sub

Public Sub Move(oForm As Form, Index As Integer, _
    dx As Long, dy As Long)

End Sub

Public Function Intersects(oForm As Form, _
    Index As Integer, x As Long, y As Long, _
    offsetX As Long, offsetY As Long) As Boolean

End Function
```

From the interface, you can see that with each method call, the client application must pass certain state-specific information to the object. It must pass the form that the asteroid will be drawn on, and usually the index of the control displaying the asteroid. The Move method passes the change in coordinates that must be made to move the asteroid to its current direction.

The FlyweightFactory is implemented using the collection object within VB:

```
Private Rocks As Collection

Public Function GetFlyweight(State As astState) As IAsteroidFlyweight
    Dim iRock As IAsteroidFlyweight

On Error Resume Next
    Select Case State
        Case LargeRock
            Set iRock = Rocks.Item("Large")
            If iRock Is Nothing Then
                Set iRock = New AsteroidsFlyweight
                iRock.State = LargeRock
                Rocks.Add iRock, "Large"
            End If
```

```
        Case MediumRock
            Set iRock = Rocks.Item("Medium")
            If iRock Is Nothing Then
                Set iRock = New AsteroidsFlyweight
                iRock.State = MediumRock
                Rocks.Add iRock, "Medium"
            End If
        Case SmallRock
            Set iRock = Rocks.Item("Small")
            If iRock Is Nothing Then
                Set iRock = New AsteroidsFlyweight
                iRock.State = SmallRock
                Rocks.Add iRock, "Small"
            End If
    End Select

    Set GetFlyweight = iRock
End Function
```

The client object makes a call to the GetFlyweight method, passing the state of the rock it wishes to retrieve. The factory checks the collection to see if the object exists and then either returns the existing object or instantiates a new flyweight and returns that.

The form plays the role of the client object in this example. The form stores the state of all of the objects. The current position is stored within the picture box control, while the direction and the speed of the rocks are stored in an array. The animation of the rocks is handled by the flyweight's move method. The MoveRocks method in the form calls the flyweight's move method each time a timer event fires, as detailed below:

```
Private Sub moveRocks()
    Dim i As Integer
    For i = 0 To UBound(Rocks) - 1
        Set oRock = oFactory.GetFlyweight(Rocks(i).State)
        oRock.Move Rocks(i).Index, Rocks(i).dx, Rocks(i).dy
    Next
End Sub
```

As you can see, the MoveRocks method just receives a reference to the flyweight object from the factory and then asks the flyweight to move the rock by passing in the extrinsic state of the asteroid.

Related Patterns

The flyweight pattern is closely related to three other patterns, the state pattern, the composite pattern, and the factory method. You can implement the state pattern as a flyweight when the criteria of the flyweight pattern are met. That is, when there are a large number of objects being instantiated and the state of those objects can be divided into intrinsic state and extrinsic state.

Whereas the state and flyweight patterns perform the same function, the flyweight pattern is often combined with the composite pattern to implement the leaf nodes of a hierarchical structure with shared objects. The document editor is a good example of this. The document editor can contain composite objects that represent the document, sections of formatting, and the characters themselves. This hierarchy of objects implemented as composite objects would simplify the interface for the document editor, and the flyweight pattern would be used to reduce the number of objects used. Combining the two allows you to create a simple and efficient document editor.

Finally, the flyweight factory uses the factory method to create new flyweight objects. In the Asteriods example, the GetFlyweight function is an example of a factory method. It allows clients to receive a reference to an already instantiated object or it creates a new object and passes that reference back to the client.

NOTE   Read more about related patterns in Chapter 6, "The Composite Pattern," Chapter 21, "The State Pattern" and Chapter 23, "The Factory Pattern."

Conclusion

The flyweight pattern is useful when implementing a large number of objects whose states can be made extrinsic to the object. By moving the state out of the object and only passing a specific state into the object to perform a function, you greatly reduce the number of objects needed to represent all of the contexts. This pattern will come in especially handy with Internet applications since the idea behind developing Internet components is that the state should be externalized to client objects like a Web browser.

chapter 10

The Proxy Pattern

- Types of proxy patterns

- A UML diagram of a proxy pattern

- A sample use of a proxy pattern

- Other uses of a proxy

- Related patterns

The *proxy* pattern works as a surrogate object that intercepts method calls to another object. It acts like a placeholder for an object that can be used to efficiently control access to another object. The proxy mimics the other object in the sense that the client does not normally know that it is communicating with a proxy.

Types of Proxy Patterns

There are three types of proxy patterns, the *remote proxy*, the *virtual proxy*, and the *protection proxy*. These proxy patterns are used in many different kinds of applications. For example, if you have ever programmed COM objects and used MTS or DCOM, then you have unknowingly created proxy objects. COM uses a set of objects called the *proxy* and *stub* to perform the out-of-process communication in DCOM. In doing this, Microsoft has freed the programmer from having to program different components for in-process objects than for out-of-process objects.

The Remote Proxy

In COM, the client application makes a call for a DCOM component. The *service control manager* (SCM) of Windows receives the call for a component and looks up the location of the component. If the component is located on another computer, the call is forwarded to the other computer's SCM. The SCM instantiates the object and returns a reference to a stub object. On the client machine, a proxy object is instantiated and a reference to this proxy is returned to the client. All communication between the client and the DCOM component is routed through the proxy and stub objects. The proxy object implements the same interface as the server object, so the client does not know that it is communicating with a component on another computer. This type of proxy is called the remote proxy.

The Virtual Proxy

Another type of proxy can be found in the Microsoft Office products. Try inserting an Excel chart into a Word document. When you insert the object and move off of it, you basically see a bitmap of the chart. The instance of Microsoft Chart has closed. Now double click on the chart to instantiate the chart object again. The bitmap of the chart acts as a proxy for the chart object. It caches information about the chart like its size and the image of the chart. When the user wants to perform some action on the chart, the proxy instantiates the chart object and forwards messages to the chart object. By implementing the proxy pattern in the Office

products, Microsoft is able to efficiently open office documents and delay the process of instantiating large objects until they are needed. This type of proxy pattern
is called the virtual proxy.

The Protection Proxy

A third type of proxy is called the protection proxy. This type of proxy provides
access control to the real object. It can restrict or grant a user access to the object
based on different access rights. DCOM also implements a type of protection
proxy inside the DCOM libraries. Within DCOM, an administrator can assign
access rights to the different DCOM servers. When a client application tries to
instantiate the object, DCOM authenticates the call using a security provider like
NT LAN Manager (NTLM). If the client is authenticated, then the user is granted
access to the DCOM server.

A UML Diagram of a Proxy Pattern

Figure 10.1 depicts a class diagram of the proxy pattern. It shows that the real subject and the proxy inherit from an abstract subject. Therefore both the real subject
and the proxy subject implement the same interface. All methods of the proxy forward a request to the real subject. This implies that the proxy must also maintain a
reference to the real subject. In turn, the reference to the real subject would be
implemented as a private variable within the proxy object.

FIGURE 10.1
A class diagram of the
proxy pattern

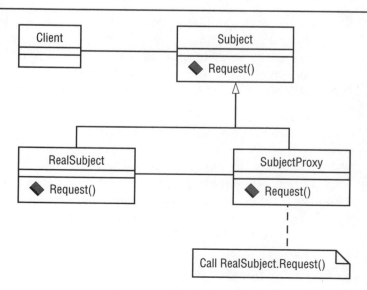

A sequence diagram depicting the proxy pattern is shown in Figure 10.2.

FIGURE 10.2
A sequence diagram of the
proxy pattern

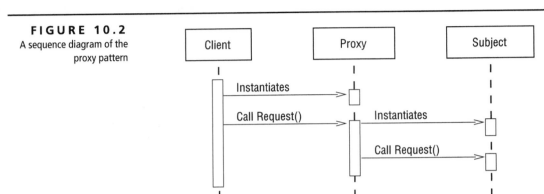

As you can see from the diagram, the proxy just forwards the requests to the subject. This level of indirection also allows you to perform certain actions whenever the request is made. The protection proxy takes advantage of this level of indirection by first authenticating the client. The virtual proxy takes advantage of this by providing *just-in-time* instantiation of the subject, as is depicted in the diagram. The instantiation of the subject is delayed until the client requests an operation.

A Sample Use of a Proxy Pattern

The following implementation of the proxy pattern is used for offline access to a database. The sample, as shown in Figure 10.3, uses the proxy pattern as a buffer to prevent the client application from knowing whether the system is connected to the server. It provides a method of storing the information locally when the application is offline. When online, the sample will connect to the real subject object.

FIGURE 10.3
A class diagram for the
sample application

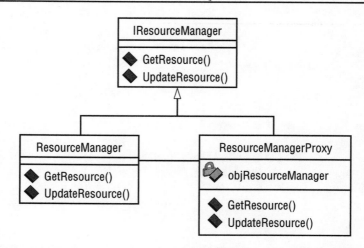

FIGURE 10.3
A class diagram for the
sample application

The sample contains three classes, an abstract interface named IResourceManager, a proxy object named ResourceManagerProxy, and the real subject object, ResourceManager. The ResourceManager would be a DCOM object running under MTS on a remote server. ResourceManagerProxy would be implemented with the client application. All of the interesting code is contained in the ResourceManagerProxy. The following code shows the implementation of the ResourceManagerProxy:

```
Implements IResourceManager

Public Enum ResourceState
    stOnline
    stOffline
End Enum

Private CurrentState As ResourceState
Private objResourceManager As IResourceManager

Private Function IResourceManager_GetResource() _
    As ADODB.Recordset
    Dim rs As ADODB.Recordset

    If CurrentState = stOffline Then
        Set rs = New ADODB.Recordset
```

```
        rs.Open App.Path & "\Data\data.rs", _
            "Provider=MSPersist", , , adCmdFile

        Set IResourceManager_GetResource = rs
    Else
        Set IResourceManager_GetResource = _
            objResourceManager.GetResource
    End If
End Function

Private Sub IResourceManager_UpdateResource( _
    resource As ADODB.Recordset)
    If CurrentState = stOffline Then
        resource.Save App.Path & "\Data\data.rs", _
            adPersistXML
    Else
        objResourceManager.UpdateResource resource
    End If
End Sub
```

From the code, you can see that the proxy object forwards the calls to the ResourceManager when it is online, but stores and retrieves the information locally when it is offline.

The ResourceManager code is similar to the proxy object, but it only has to implement one state, that of being online. The code for the ResourceManager is as follows:

```
Implements IResourceManager

Private Function IResourceManager_GetResource() _
    As ADODB.Recordset
    Dim conn As ADODB.Connection
    Dim rs As ADODB.Recordset
    Dim sSQL As String

    Set conn = New ADODB.Connection
    Set rs = New ADODB.Connection

    sSQL = "SELECT * FROM products"

    conn.Open strConnection
```

```
    rs.CursorLocation = adUseClient
    rs.CursorType = adOpenStatic
    rs.LockType = adLockBatchOptimistic

    rs.Open sSQL, conn

    Set rs.ActiveConnection = Nothing
    conn.Close
    Set conn = Nothing

    Set IResourceManager_GetResource = rs
End Function

Private Sub IResourceManager_UpdateResource( _
    resource As ADODB.Recordset)
    Dim conn As New ADODB.Connection

    conn.Open sConnectionString

    Set resource.ActiveConnection = conn

    resource.UpdateBatch

    conn.Close
    Set conn = Nothing
End Sub
```

The GetResource manager simply queries the database and returns a recordset to the proxy object. The UpdateResource method receives a recordset as a parameter and updates the database by calling the UpdateBatch method of the recordset.

Other Uses of a Proxy

As mentioned, there are several different types of proxy patterns, virtual proxies, remote proxies, and protection proxies. These types of proxies can be used in a variety of applications. The virtual proxies come in handy when you want to implement just-in-time activation of a large object or a large number of objects. The virtual proxy will delay the activation of the objects until they are needed.

The protection proxy can be used to implement a security layer. For example, if the client application is not authenticated, then the protection proxy can refuse the client access to the subject objects. The sample application from above can be considered a protection proxy because it controls access to the subject objects, depending on whether a connection to the server exists or not.

Related Patterns

The proxy pattern is related to several other patterns. The protection proxy pattern is very similar to the decorator pattern and sometimes only differs in the intent. For example, the decorator pattern adds one or more responsibilities to an object, whereas the protection proxy controls access to another object.

The proxy pattern is also similar to the adapter pattern. The adapter pattern is usually implemented with a different interface than the object it is adapting. The proxy pattern, on the other hand, implements the same interface. In addition, the adapter pattern can be used to transform an interface from an object so it conforms to another set of objects. In contrast, the proxy pattern is used to provide a level of indirection that allows for more flexible software.

The facade pattern is similar to the proxy in that it encapsulates other objects, but the facade is used to unify the interfaces of multiple classes in a subsystem. The facade's purpose is to simplify an interface to a subsystem. It is not meant to do anything other than recast the interface. The proxy provides another level within the code to perform certain actions like just-in-time activation or authentication

---

NOTE   Read more about related patterns in Chapter 5, "The Adapter Pattern," Chapter 7, "The Decorator Pattern," and Chapter 8, "The Facade Pattern."

Conclusion

The proxy pattern is used whenever you need an object to receive method calls on behalf of another object. It can be used to delay the activation of large objects or the opening of files until they are needed. It can also be used to control access to objects, so method calls are authenticated prior to calling the subject objects.

PART III

Behavioral Patterns

chapter 11

The Observer Pattern

■ Types of observer patterns

■ A UML diagram of an observer pattern

■ Using a push observer pattern

■ Other uses of an observer

■ Overcoming limitations to an observer pattern

■ Related patterns

The *observer* pattern allows you to flexibly design interaction between any number of objects, allowing one object to handle the client calls, while deciding at run time which other capabilities to call. Think of using an observer pattern whenever you have a relationship between one particular event or action and many possible results.

These patterns are most useful when you need to communicate among multiple objects in a changing and flexible manner. Observers allow objects to interact, either by having observers register themselves with their subjects (passive/push observers) or by having the observer poll for information from its subject (voyeur/pull observers). The key is that these patterns allow objects to turn on and off their interest in subjects at run time.

Types of Observer Patterns

Observer Patterns define a one-to-many dependency between objects. So, when one object changes state, all of its dependents are notified and updated automatically. There are two main implementations of observers, *pull observers* and *push observers*. The difference between the two is in how the observer relates to its subject or subjects, and in how much data is passed from the subject to the observer.

Pull Observers

A pull observer is an *active* observer that pulls in the state of its subjects. In Visual Basic, this is often done with a raised event or with a timer. Pull observers are sometimes known as *voyeurs*. In this model, when an event occurs, minimal information flows between a subject and its observer. The observer then has to get any information that it requires.

For instance, if you are writing a front end to a swimming pool monitoring system, you would want to track the temperature of the pool, as well as the height of the water. Your system might employ a timer (the pull observer) that fires every few minutes to check subjects that track these figures. It would then call out to client objects, which would handle adjusting the temperature and water level accordingly. In this case, your pull observer knows what to check, and who to call if there's a change. It doesn't handle what to do, however. That is left up to the client, which can be modified as necessary. The pull observer tends to be very reusable because it doesn't make any assumptions about the information it initially receives from a subject. On the other hand, it has to discover what changes have occurred on its own.

Push Observers

In contrast to a pull observer, a push observer is a passive observer that needs its subjects to send notification messages for the observer to perform its role of updating a client. The push observer is also known by the name *publish-and-subscribe*. In this model, the subject sends over all the information that a push observer requires when an event occurs. A push observer is useful whenever you are getting a regular flow of information from an outside data source. This can include stock ticker information across a serial port, a news feed from the Internet, or regular data updates from a scheduled database query.

Let's take as an example a news feed from the Internet. In the application you are designing, you want the client to be alerted whenever certain keywords appear in a story. You could design the application to pass every story to multiple objects, which then test for their assigned keywords. Or, you could make each object register with a central observer, sending the observer only the keywords that they care about. The central observer checks the Internet news feed for all the keywords. It alerts only the one appropriate object of its keyword findings, thus passing to each object the information it needs to do its work.

Each object then acts on its own to do what is required—pop up a window alerting you, e-mailing you a copy of the story for later, or whatever the object needs to do. The push observer knows only enough about the subscriber to pass along the required information. Note that the push observer doesn't know what to do with the information. It merely notifies its subscribers about the information change. It is up to the client to choose how to publish the information.

The push observer tends to be more tightly bound to its subject than the pull observer, in that the interface between them contains more information. However, it also tends to be more efficient than the pull observer, since it can trust on having the information that it needs and therefore there is less polling between objects.

A UML Diagram of an Observer Pattern

As you can see from the UML class diagram in Figure 11.1, we are working with two basic classes, subject and observer. A subject can have any number of observers that depend on it. Each observer, when notified that something has changed, either queries the subject directly, or receives information from the subject (and then acts upon that information). The difference between the pull and push observer, at its simplest level, is the amount of data passed as parameters to the `Observer.Update` call.

Let's look at the diagram in more detail. A subject is connected and disconnected from the observer via the attach and detach methods. In this manner, the two objects can communicate with each other. When something happens externally to the system, the observer is notified through its Update method. The observer can then send information to any subject that it needs to. It can also gather information from one subject to pass to others through the subject's Notify method.

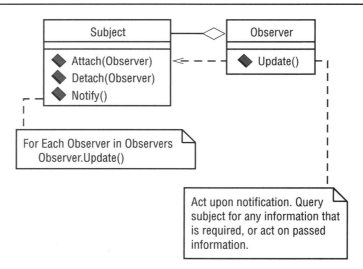

FIGURE 11.1
A UML diagram of a generic observer

Using a Push Observer Pattern

Let's assume that you are writing a system with multiple windows that have to be kept updated in a coordinated fashion. For instance, say you are receiving information about the value of a stock, and when that stock hits a certain value, you need to update all of the windows with the new value. You could approach updating the information in two different ways:

- Write the code with hard-coded window references to update all of the windows that are necessary.

- Write the code so that any window that needs the information informs a centralized object of its interest.

The second approach is obviously more flexible because it allows each window to "know" which events it is interested in, post its interest in the event, and receive the information when necessary. Figure 11.2 shows a sample application.

FIGURE 11.2
A sample application window

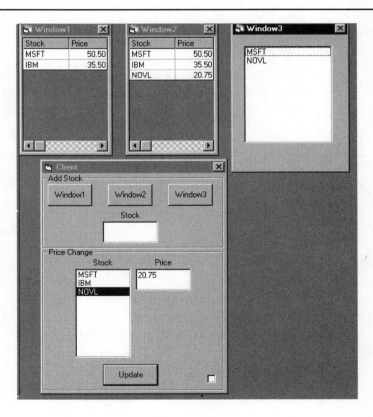

The sample application includes three forms that track stock information. For this example, the forms are set up as shown in Table 11.1.

TABLE 11.1: Forms and the Stocks they are interested in

Form	Stocks of Interest
Form1	MSFT IBM
Form2	MSFT IBM NOVL
Form3	MSFT NOVL

When a new price is entered for a stock, the Update method of the subject is called, which then iterates through its collection of observers, calling the observers' Publish methods. Each observer is responsible for responding to the call in its own manner using a bridge pattern.

> **NOTE**   See Chapter 4: "The Bridge Pattern," to learn how to create three kinds of bridge patterns.

Figure 11.3 shows a class design for this application. As you can see, we create an interface called Ipublisher, which standardizes our methods for all the forms that we'll use in our application. When we get a new stock price, the Update method of the subject calls the Publish method of each form. Each form can then handle displaying the data as it sees fit.

FIGURE 11.3
A stock tracking observer

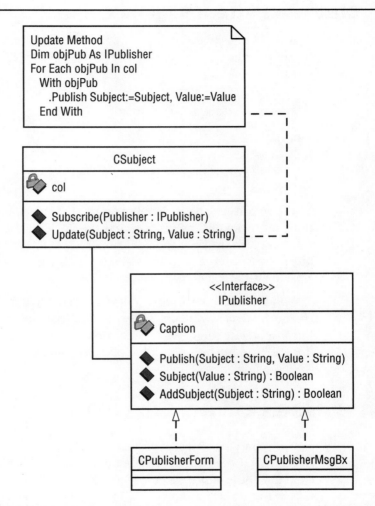

```
Update Method
Dim objPub As IPublisher
For Each objPub In col
  With objPub
    .Publish Subject:=Subject, Value:=Value
  End With
End With
```

CSubject

🔒 col

◆ Subscribe(Publisher : IPublisher)
◆ Update(Subject : String, Value : String)

<<Interface>>
IPublisher

🔒 Caption

◆ Publish(Subject : String, Value : String)
◆ Subject(Value : String) : Boolean
◆ AddSubject(Subject : String) : Boolean

CPublisherForm

CPublisherMsgBx

The CSubject class gets any information regarding new stock pricing from the client. It then calls the various publishers' Publish method. That method checks to see if it is interested in the subject that was passed, and if so, acts upon it.

Observer Pattern Sample Code

The following sample code shows how the push pattern works, from the perspective of the client. In this example, goSubject is the object that references the subject class:

```
'Price of stock changes
Private Sub cmdUpdate_Click()
If Trim(txtPrice) = "" Or lstStock.ListIndex = -1 Then _
  Exit Sub
goSubject.Update _
    lstStock.List(lstStock.ListIndex), txtPrice.Text
End Sub
```

As you can see, the click of the update button is fairly clear. As long as we have filled in a price and a stock, we pass the stock identifier and the price to the subject. That's all an application developer has to know. The subject handles notifying any and all observer windows about the change. The windows then show the stock prices in the manner in which they were designed.

With this code, we achieve a flexible system where events (like stock price changes) are passed to one observer. At the same time, other objects subscribe to the observer, telling it when they wish to be notified. In this manner, each form does not need to be constantly polling our stock ticker information.

Other Uses of an Observer

You will find the observer pattern useful when you want to update any User Interface (UI) element because some sort of data—or the property of an object—changes. For instance, as people enter information into your VB application, you may want to auto-update an Excel spreadsheet or a charting object that is open in another window. This allows the user to see their data immediately update when they use your application.

You can also use the observer pattern to create a summary of information that has been gathered from sources throughout a company. By allowing uncommon changes to inform your application of the change, you can lessen the amount of polling that takes place to gather information. For instance, let's assume that accounting information changes daily, but sales commissions are calculated monthly. Instead of checking to see if salesman commissions have been updated every day on application startup, you can create a salesman commission observer that notifies your application when the values change, passing the totals to your application. This can greatly reduce network traffic. Observer patterns are very useful in Executive Information System (EIS) types of applications. You can add new methods of both gathering information and displaying the information, without modifying other pieces of your application.

Overcoming Limitations to an Observer Pattern

Due to its run time flexibility, the Observer pattern is susceptible to problems with circular references to the observers. To avoid memory leaks, you must explicitly tell the subject to release the registered observers when it is destroyed.

In addition, when creating observers, focus on the interface between the subject and the observers. In particular, take care when you decide how much information should be passed from the subject to the observer. You can create very generic observer patterns where the observer not only registers itself with the subject, but also passes to the event it is interested in. The more generic you make the implementation of the pattern, the more complex (and occasionally slower) it can get.

Related Patterns

As a related pattern, mediator patterns often consist of smart observer patterns. In other words, they mediate between multiple observers, handling the logic of which observer actually has to be informed of an event. In this case, your observer becomes smart, in that it controls the subjects that it is alerting. Instead of alerting a subject when something changes, it has the knowledge of which particular objects to alert and in what order, so that you can centralize complex communication between objects.

NOTE   Read more about the mediator pattern in Chapter 12.

Conclusion

Observer patterns allow you to flexibly design interaction between any number of objects, allowing one object to handle the client calls, while deciding at run time which other objects need to be called. Any time you have a one-to-many relation between numerous objects, look at cleaning up the relations through the use of observer patterns.

The Mediator Pattern

- Types of mediator patterns

- A UML diagram of a mediator pattern

- A sample use of a mediator pattern

- Other uses of a mediator

- Related patterns

The *mediator* pattern is one of the most useful and commonly used patterns. In Visual Basic, it is used most often in the New Form window, where the form mediates for its component controls. The mediator pattern consists of an object (the mediator) that acts like a traffic cop, controlling the interaction between a set of objects. The mediator encapsulates the rules of interaction between the set of objects. This is accomplished by loosely coupling the objects. As a result, the objects are not aware of each other: they are only aware of the mediator object. All traffic goes through the mediator. Mediator patterns are best used when you have a complex grouping of objects that have to communicate with each other.

Types of Mediator Patterns

There is only one basic type of mediator. It always consists of an object that manages the communication of a complex group of objects. However, the specific-shape the mediator takes can change depending on the situation. The mediator may communicate to various objects in ways that are similar to other patterns—but the fact that the mediator controls the communication makes it a mediator. For example, the mediator pattern is often implemented as an observer pattern, where the mediator is notified of changes that occur. However, instead of just passing that information to its colleagues (as an observer would), the mediator does something with the information. It acts appropriately to the situation.

In this case, for example, you could have a mediator object responsible for communicating to all forms that are currently visible on a screen, and is an observer for any data changes, letting the appropriate forms know what is happening. Consider the following scenario: a customer form is visible on the computer screen, as is an invoice form that shows the invoices for a customer. The user presses the delete button on the customer form. The customer form tells the mediator that customer John Smith has just been deleted. The mediator could then, based on certain rules, broadcast the fact that customer Smith was deleted to all visible forms. All these visible forms would then determine whether they are currently displaying information about Smith, and if so, the forms are released from memory. The mediator is unaware of the action that the notified forms will take. The mediator just serves as a communication hub, notifying every object that needs to know something has changed.

NOTE   The mediator pattern is very useful for Visual Basic programmers because it is a way of working around the lack of inheritance. We create many objects that provide colleague capability, and a mediator handles the behavior. Our colleagues do not have to use inheritance to modify behavior. This pattern also enhances reuse of a system, since colleagues and mediators can be used independently and across applications.

A UML Diagram of a Mediator Pattern

As you can see from the interaction diagram in Figure 12.1, all four of the colleagues communicate with the mediator to accomplish some process. This allows you to have a centralized place for manipulation of processes that may regularly change. If any of the colleague objects need something, they make a request of the mediator, and the mediator handles the request. In turn, the mediator forwards the request to the appropriate object. That object processes the request, and returns the results to the mediator. The mediator then returns the results to the original object. In this scenario, all communications go through the mediator. This centralization helps with proper encapsulation of knowledge in objects. With the mediator pattern, colleagues do not talk to each other; they only talk to the mediator.

FIGURE 12.1
An interaction diagram of a
mediator pattern

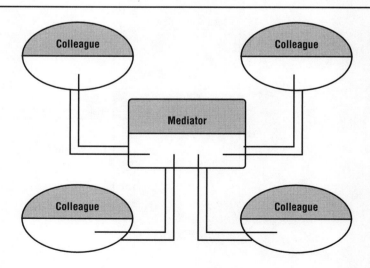

Let's say, for example, you want to create a mediator object that knows how to calculate the total of all of the invoices for a customer. You look at your object model, and you notice that you have a customer bizobj that knows how to find a particular customer record based on a social security number, and an invoice bizobj that knows how to find the invoice records that belong to a particular customer id. To take advantage of the knowledge already encapsulated in these objects (reuse), the mediator asks the customer bizobj for a customer (using a social security number). The customer bizobj returns a customer to the mediator. The mediator reads the customer id, and then passes the customer id to the invoices bizobj, which returns a group of invoices to the mediator. The mediator then totals the value of the group of invoices. The mediator prevents the need to tightly couple the customer bizobj and the invoice bizobj. In fact, different applications may have different rules for how customers and invoices interact. These rules can be encapsulated in mediators, leaving the customer and invoice objects more available for reuse. Mediators of this sort are a wonderful way of coding business processes in a component-based system. Figure 12.2 is a sample sequence diagram for the invoice totaling process.

FIGURE 12.2
A sequence diagram for invoice totaling process.

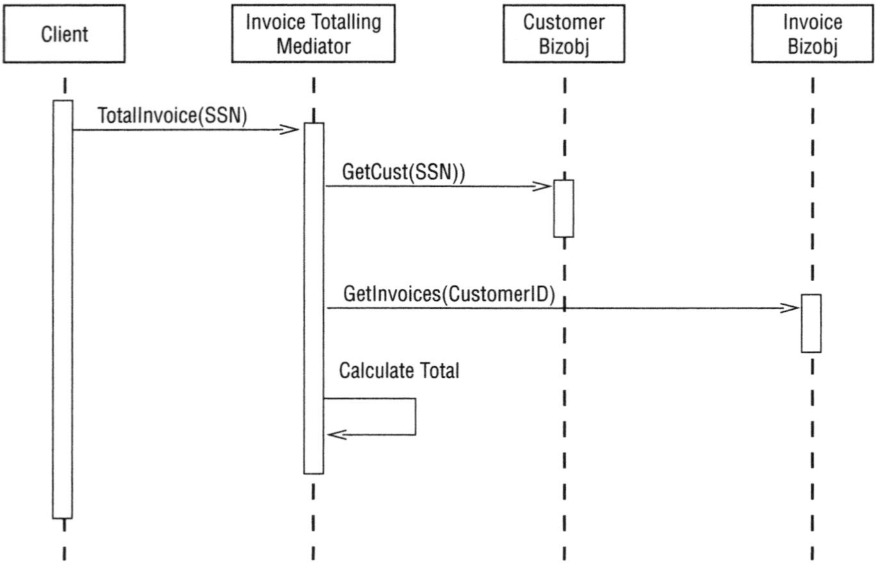

Note from the diagram that the client calls the mediator; it doesn't know about the various business objects. As a result, you can replace the approach used to total the invoices without affecting the core components of your application, the business objects and the client forms.

Using a Mediator Pattern

Now that we've seen a UML diagram of a mediator pattern, let's look at the code for a mediator. This example will probably be one of those "but of course you do it that way" pieces of code. And that's exactly the point of a design pattern. Design patterns are natural solutions to recurring problems. Therefore, the fact that you get the "of course" feeling simply means that you've been using the pattern all along. This example will provide sample code for a form where certain controls need to be enabled or disabled, based on the values of other controls. Instead of putting the code in the controls, we'll use the form as a mediator, having one procedure that controls a particular aspect of the form.

Here are two samples of the form at work.

FIGURE 12.3
Our sample form set to Buy
with no stock selected

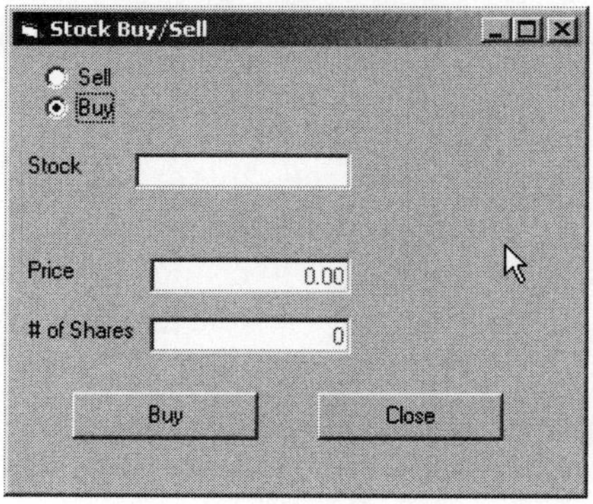

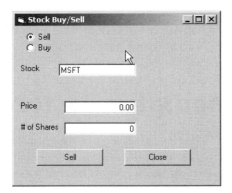

Note that in Figure 12.3, the Price and # of Shares textboxes are disabled, and the command button's caption is set to Buy. Figure 12.4 has the textboxes enabled, with the button set to Sell. Our rules for this form's interface state that we should only allow entry into Price and # of Shares if a stock is selected. We should also set the command button to mirror the option that the user has selected.

Mediator Pattern Sample Code

Instead of putting the code for the interface rules in both the option buttons and the Stocks textbox, we place it in one procedure and let the form act as the mediator. Note that VB always uses the form as a mediator. All VB code is in the form, not the object. However, this sample uses a custom control, and the encapsulation of that control's code leads us to use a mediator. This will allow us to drop the control on any form, but change what happens during the changed event on any form. Here's the code for the user control:

```
Public Event Changed()
Private strCommand As String
Private Property Let command(strValue As String)
    strCommand = strValue
End Property
Property Get command() As String
    command = strCommand
End Property
Private Sub optBuySell_Click(Index As Integer)
    command = IIf(Index = 0, "Sell", "Buy")
    RaiseEvent Changed
End Sub
```

Note that the above code simply defines a property Command that can be queried to get whichever option button is currently selected, and an event Changed that can be used by the host of the custom control.

Here's the mediator code:

```
Private Sub FormLookAndFeelMediator()

'Enable price and shares only when stock entered
If txtStock.Text <> "" Then
    txtPrice.Enabled = True
    txtShares.Enabled = True
Else
    txtPrice.Enabled = False
    txtShares.Enabled = False
End If

'Change the caption based on the option group
cmdBuySell.Caption = usrBuySell1.command
```

Other Uses of a Mediator

In addition to using mediators to handle a business process in a component-based system, mediators can be used in the following situations.

Database Driven Decisions

Mediators can use database information to decide which objects should be instantiated for a given situation. For instance, let's assume that we are writing a system for a cable television company. When a customer signs up for a package of pay stations, the cable company gets charged by the television stations for telling each station to sign up or remove a customer. The cable company could take the order for the new package and, at the same time, delete the prior package. However, any duplication will cause a double charge to the cable company (once for removing a pay channel, once for adding that same channel). On the other hand, we can have the order-taking process call a mediator. The mediator will ask the old package object for a list of its stations, then will ask the new package object for a list of its stations, finally creating a set of delete and add orders that avoid duplication, thereby saving the cable company a lot of money.

Inheritance Work-around

The mediator pattern is very useful for Visual Basic programmers because it is a way of working around the lack of inheritance. We create many objects that provide colleague capability, and a mediator handles the behavior. Our colleagues do not have to use inheritance to modify behavior. This pattern also enhances reuse of a system since colleagues and mediators can be used independently and across applications. While the mediator class itself can be harder to maintain and reuse, the system of colleagues that the mediator works with can be more easily reused because they are more self-contained.

User Interface Creation

Mediators are also very useful in user interface creation. If you have multiple controls that rely on each other (for instance, disable *control A* if *control B* is selected), you can use the form itself as a mediator. Each control would let the form know it has changed. The form would then let the other controls know what change has occurred. This allows us to drop the controls on many forms, without worrying that behavior from one form will affect another.

Related Patterns

Mediators provide two-way communication from the parts to the mediator and back. Facade patterns differ from mediators in that they provide unidirectional communication from the facade to the parts it is hiding.

Colleague to mediator communication is often implemented using the observer pattern. In this approach, a colleague would broadcast any changes to its mediator by treating the mediator as an observer. In this manner, the mediator is informed when changes occur, and based on those changes, can tell other colleagues to act appropriately.

NOTE   Learn more about these related patterns in Chapter 8, "Facade," and Chapter 11, "Observer."

Conclusion

The mediator pattern is one of the most useful and commonly used patterns. It is typically used in forms where the form mediates for its component controls. Moreover, in a component-based architecture, the mediator emulates business processes. The main downside to the mediator pattern is that the mediator class becomes more complex (since it contains all the behavioral code). As a result, this class can be harder to maintain and reuse. However, the benefits from decoupling objects using the mediator far outweighs the increase complexity for the mediator class.

chapter 13

The Chain of Responsibility Pattern

- An example of a chain of responsibility pattern

- A UML diagram of a chain of responsibility pattern

- A sample use of a chain of responsibility pattern

- Other uses of a chain of responsibility

- Related patterns

The *chain of responsibility* pattern is an extremely flexible and extensible pattern. Chain of responsibility decouples the sender of a request from its receiver by giving more than one object a chance to handle the request. The request is passed along a group—or chain—of objects.

This pattern is useful in a variety of situations. For example, you can use the chain of responsibility pattern when more than one object can handle a request, but the requesting object does not know which object should answer the request. This pattern is also useful when the programmer does not want to directly specify which object will handle a particular request, for instance when any number of objects can handle a request depending on the situation. Instead of a giant Select Case statement, the object can decide for itself. You might also use this pattern when the objects used to handle a request need to be specified dynamically—in other words, when the elements of the chain can vary.

Chains of responsibility allow you to create a very granular architecture (many little classes) that can be assembled in many different ways. This distribution of functionality can be very helpful with object reuse because each small object can be reused since it does only one thing. Note that it is not necessary for a chain of responsibility to stop processing a request when it hits the first appropriate object during the chain; it can continue down the chain, allowing all objects to handle the request.

An Example of a Chain of Responsibility Pattern

Steven Black's INTL is a product that provides international localization capabilities to source code. This product uses a chain of responsibility to *internationalize* various aspects of the objects that you create. Any object being internationalized by INTL is passed through the entire chain. When INTL internationalizes a label object on the screen, for instance, the label object is passed to a chain of responsibility that contains strategy objects. The first strategy object in the chain translates (among other things) the caption of the label. The next strategy object in the chain changes the font of the label object. INTL allows you to add strategy objects to this chain at run time. This allows the developer the opportunity to extend INTL without changing INTL's code.

NOTE   For more on the strategy pattern, see Chapter 22.

For example, you could create a strategy that modifies the color of an object based on the country to which you are shipping your application. INTL has methods for adding a new strategy to the chain at run time, so you are able to add this new strategy to INTL. Now INTL knows how to internationalize your applications, without having to change INTL itself. A benefit of this run-time configuration is that the developer does not necessarily need to have the source code of INTL to change its behavior. The developer just needs to create classes that conform to INTL's programming interfaces, and register them with INTL. Thus, chain of responsibility patterns are excellent for inserting run-time flexibility at predictable junctures in code.

A UML Diagram of a Chain of Responsibility Pattern

As you can see from Figure 13.1, a chain of responsibility simply consists of an object that has a reference to another object with the same interface. It typically has methods that allow it to dynamically point to the next object on the list, and to execute some operation. When the Execute method is called, the message is passed from one object to another along the chain. When the message is handled, the handling object has the option of one, stopping the chain (by not passing the message on), or two, continuing to pass the message along the chain, thereby allowing other objects to act upon it.

FIGURE 13.1
A UML diagram of an abstract chain of responsibility class

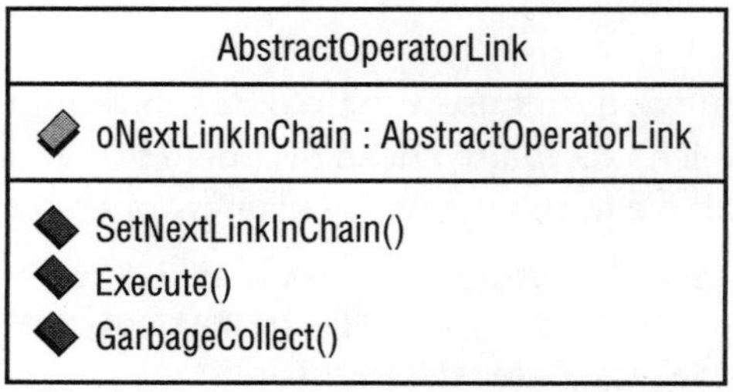

AbstractOperatorLink
◆ oNextLinkInChain : AbstractOperatorLink
◆ SetNextLinkInChain() ◆ Execute() ◆ GarbageCollect()

A chain of responsibility class will often have some sort of explicit *garbage collection* method. This method cleans up the object references down the chain, so that all of the memory used by the chain is cleared.

A Sample Use of a Chain of Responsibility Pattern

Suppose you want to create a calculator class that has an Execute method that accepts two operands and an operator, and returns the result of the operation. With an eye toward future functionality, you want to be able to easily add new operators to the calculator, without having to change the programming interface of the calculator object (for example, add methods/code for each new operator). The calculator class could be configured with a chain of "operator" link objects that will each be given a chance to handle the operands and return a result.

Figure 13.2 is a diagram of the operator link hierarchy. As you can see, when the calculator calls its Execute method (makes the request), it does not know which of the links in the chain (AdditionLink, SubtractionLink, and so on) will handle the calculation.

FIGURE 13.2
A UML diagram of the
calculator and its chain of
responsibility

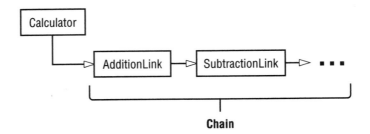

If we didn't use a chain of responsibility, the calculator would have to know which link to use ahead of time. This would force the calculator's Execute method to have to change with each new operator link created, as in the code below:

```
Sub CalculateAmt(strOperator,intOperand1,intOperand2)
' THIS IS AN EXAMPLE OF WHAT WE ARE TRYING TO AVOID '
Select Case strOperator
Case  "+"
```

```
            CalculateAmt = _
            oAdditionLink.Calculate( _
            intOperand1,intOperand2)
    Case "-"
            CalculateAmt = _
            oSubtractionLink.Calculate( _
            intOperand1,intOperand2)
    ...
    End Select
    End Sub
```

Remember, the goal is to decouple the calculator (as the requestor) from the object that handles the request. In the above code, every new operator will require a change to the Select Case statement, forcing us to recompile our code each time.

With a chain of responsibility, to make the calculator understand a new operation, you merely add a new class that adheres to the AbstractOperatorLink interface to the chain. Different applications can configure this same calculator object with different operator objects. A scientific application may need geometrical functions (SIN, COS, TAN), while a recipe application may require conversions (teaspoon to tablespoon, pound to ounces), and so on. The chain of responsibility's class diagram is shown in Figure 13.3.

FIGURE 13.3
The calculator class
hierarchy

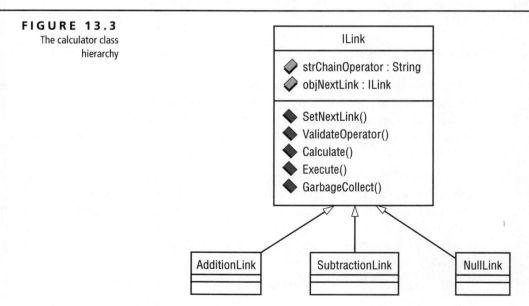

As you can see from the class hierarchy, every operator is based on the Ilink interface. Table 13.1 describes all of the properties and methods of the class.

TABLE 13.1: The properties and methods of the ILink interface class.

Property	Description
strChainOperator	Operator that the class understands (+, -, etcetera)
objNextLink	Object reference to the next operator object that will have a chance to handle the request if this object cannot

Method (parameters)	Description
SetNextLink(objOperator As ILink)	Public sub that adds the passed operator object to the end of the chain
ValidateOperator (strOperator As String) As Boolean	Private function that determines whether the operator class knows how to handle the calculation, based on the operator passed.
Calculate (vOperator As Variant, vOperand1 As Variant, vOperand2 As Variant) As Variant	Private function that performs the operation on the operands and returns the result.
Execute(vOperator As Variant, vOperand1 As Variant, vOperand2 As Variant) As Variant	Public function that passes an operator and operands to the chain's calculate methods. **This is all the client has to know about the interface to the chain.**

The chain is maintained using the objNextLink property. Notice that not only is the chain used to execute the operation (Execute), but also the GarbageCollect method. The GarbageCollect message travels all the way down the chain, and on its way back up the chain the link is nulled out. This prevents dangling object references.

The heart of this class is the Execute method. The Calculator calls Execute on the first operator object in the chain. If the operator object knows how to handle the operator, it calls its own Calculate method and returns the result back up the chain to the requesting object (the Calculator). If it does not know how to handle the calculation, it tries to pass the request to the next link in the chain via the Execute method.

Below is the calculate code for the AdditionLink and SubtractionLink classes, which allows the calculator to understand the + operator and the - operator, respectively. Note that cAbstractOperatorLink is the class that implements the interface.

```vb
'This is for the Addition class
Private Function cAbstractOperatorLink_Calculate( _
    ByVal vOperator As Variant, _
    ByVal vOperand1 As Variant, _
    ByVal vOperand2 As Variant) As Variant


If Not IsNumeric(vOperand1) Or _
    Not IsNumeric(vOperand2) Then

    cAbstractOperatorLink_Calculate = _
        "Operands must be numeric values."
Else
    'each link has its own "operator" sign
    cAbstractOperatorLink_Calculate = _
            CDbl(vOperand1) + CDbl(vOperand2)
End If
End Function

'This is for the subtraction class
Private Function cAbstractOperatorLink_Calculate( _
        ByVal vOperator As Variant, _
        ByVal vOperand1 As Variant, _
        ByVal vOperand2 As Variant) As Variant
If Not IsNumeric(vOperand1) Or _
    Not IsNumeric(vOperand2) Then

    cAbstractOperatorLink_Calculate = _
            "Operands must be numeric values."
Else
    'each link has its own "operator" sign
    cAbstractOperatorLink_Calculate = _
            CDbl(vOperand1) - CDbl(vOperand2)
End If
End Function
```

Notice that the code for the two links in the chain is very similar. In fact, the code only differs in the exact operation itself. Chains of responsibility will often show this pattern. Every link in the chain is easy to create because it only focuses on accomplishing one thing. In this case, one operation.

Let's take a quick look at the Execute method. This is the method that actually uses the chain. It checks first to see if it understands the operator that was passed (using the ValidateOperator method). If so, it calls the Calculate method and the call ends. If it does not know how to handle the operator, it checks to see if there's another link in the chain, and if so, passes the call along to that link's Execute method.

```
Public Function cAbstractOperatorLink_Execute(ByVal vOperator, _
        ByVal vOperand1, ByVal vOperand2)

If poParent.ValidateOperator(vOperator) Then
        Execute = poParent.Calculate(vOperator, vOperand1, vOperand2)
Else
    If Not poNextLinkInChain Is Nothing Then
        Execute = poNextLinkInChain.Execute(vOperator, _
        vOperand1, vOperand2)
        Else
        Execute = "No match for the operator was found."
        End If
End If

End Function
```

Note also that the GarbageCollect method works the same way. It checks to see if there is a link in the chain, calling down the chain until it reaches the end. At this point, it begins setting the NextLinkInChain property to Nothing, clearing the chain from the end up to the beginning.

Finally, let's look at how we build the chain in our calculator class.

```
Public Sub BuildOperatorChain()
'Build the chain
Dim Obj As cAbstractOperatorLink
Set oOperatorChain = New cNullLink
Set Obj = New cAdditionLink
oOperatorChain.SetNextLinkInChain Obj
Set Obj = New cSubtractionLink
oOperatorChain.SetNextLinkInChain Obj
End Sub
```

Notice the NullLink object. Its job is to be the first item in the chain. In fact, it *is* the chain, until other links are added to the chain. Its CheckOperator method always returns false, which forces the next link in the chain to try and handle the request. Imagine the flexibility of a table-driven version of BuildOperatorChain that adds operators to itself based on a table containing the names of classes that adhere to the interface of ILink!

Other Uses of a Chain of Responsibility

While there is only one type of chain of responsibility, its usage can vary. A chain of responsibility can also be used when you want to add capabilities to a routine at a future date, or when you want to flexibly model a process that may change from application to application.

Add Capabilities to a Routine

You can use the chain of responsibility pattern when you want to add more capabilities to a routine at a future date, but do not want to have to recompile or modify the routine. An example of this might include calculating sales tax in a Point of Sale application. Every state (and many cities) in the United States calculates sales tax differently. By creating a chain of Sales Tax objects that know which state or city they represent, and the appropriate calculation, you can easily calculate sales taxes as needed by calling the first link in the chain. The objects that are appropriate will add their sales tax to the total. You can add new sales tax calculations by providing more objects to the application.

Flexibly Model a Process

You can also use the chain of responsibility when you want to flexibly model a process that may change from application to application, while using many of the same basic functions. For instance, if you have to create an import routine for every application you write, then the import routine needs to perform certain functions, such as determining if the import file exists, checking if the import file contains the correct data, moving the import file into a temporary storage area, running rules on the temporary storage area, and importing to the final database. Each of these functions may be reused between different import routines, or they may have pieces that are reused between different import routines. Defining the import routine as a chain of responsibility allows you to reuse various small-grain objects between applications, while still having the flexibility to define sections of it specifically for a particular purpose.

Related Patterns

A chain of responsibility can often work with a composite. In this situation, the component's parent acts as the successor in the chain, allowing you to traverse up the composite when performing an action.

A chain of responsibility will often chain strategy classes. In this case, an application process will be put together on the fly as a chain of strategies that the application requires.

NOTE To learn more about related patterns, see Chapter 6, "The Composite Pattern," and Chapter 22, "The Strategy Pattern."

Conclusion

As a VB developer, you will find yourself using the chain of responsibility pattern often. It is an extremely flexible and extensible pattern that decouples the sender of a request from its receiver by giving more than one object a chance to handle the request. It is especially useful in COM-based systems, where capabilities are added as new DLLs register themselves with the system. The chain of responsibility thus allows you to extend capabilities in the future, without recompiling the source code or creating new release versions.

The Command Pattern

- A UML diagram of a command pattern

- A sample use of a command pattern

- Other uses of a command

- Related patterns

The *command* pattern is used to turn a client procedure call into an object. Command gives the procedure request a life of its own so that the request can have its own behaviors and properties. Once you turn a client request into a command object, you can accomplish a number of tasks. First, the command can save the request so that it can be executed at a later time. Second, the command can maintain a history list of all the times the request was called so that it can undo and redo actions or write them to a log. And third, the command can also perform any necessary preprocessing before the request is executed. The command object, then, does not carry out the request; rather it receives the request from the client, performs the functionality that it was designed to do, and then passes the request to the server object that is able to carry out the client's request.

The command pattern thus turns a procedure call into a smart object that can assist in the execution of the call. For example, suppose you want to extend an application that was designed to run on a local area network to include a front-end running on a wireless device. This front end consists of a form that runs on the wireless computer. This form calls an object on the network that writes data to the server. The problem is that the connection to the server is not always available. You can solve this problem by using the command pattern.

Instead of having the client form call directly to the server object, it should call to a command object running locally on the wireless computer. The command object can then check whether the connection is available. If it is not available, then the command should save the call and its parameters locally. You can then program a timed service run which checks for outstanding server requests and executes them by calling the server object. This connection-checking functionality is transparent to both the client and server objects. By adding the command object, you can take the same objects that run on a computer that's hooked up to a LAN and extend it to a wireless device. This example thus illustrates how the command pattern turns a procedure call into a smart object that can assist in the execution of the call.

The key to implementing the command pattern —as with many patterns—is to decouple the client and server objects so that the client does not call directly to the server object. Rather, have the client call a procedure of the command object. In that procedure, command can assist in the execution of the request, do preprocessing, or maintain a history list of calls. After command does what you designed it to do, it can then pass the call to the server object. By using this pattern, the client object does not need a reference to the server object. In some cases, you might find yourself reprogramming an existing system where the client is already bound to the server object. In that situation, you can use Visual Basic's `Implements` keyword to have command assume the interface of the server. Now, the client can be bound to the command object instead of the server object.

NOTE   Learn more about Visual Basic's `Implements` keyword in Chapter 3, "Visual Basic and Design Patterns."

A UML Diagram of a Command Pattern

As you can see from Figure 14.1, a command is an intermediary object that intercepts client procedure requests, does some preprocessing, and then delegates the execution of the request to the server object.

FIGURE 14.1
A UML diagram of a
command pattern

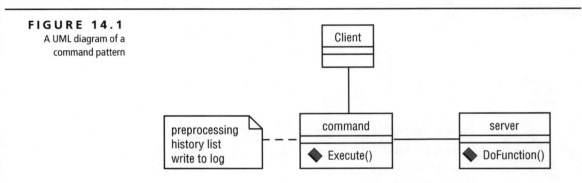

A Sample Use of a Command Pattern

For our sample, we'll create the objects for a calculator that allows the user to step backwards and forwards through calculations. The two classes that we'll work with are calculator and commandCalculator. Calculator performs the actual calculations. The command object commandCalculator maintains a history list of all the calculations, and has an Undo and Redo method that lets the user traverse the chain of calculations. Here's how it works: The client form takes the input from the user and passes it to commandCalculator. CommandCalculator stores the number and operator used in the calculation in a disconnected recordset. The recordset also has a Boolean field called Undone, which determines if the action has already been undone and therefore can be redone. CommandCalculator's Undo method finds the last action performed and reapplies it to the current total. Figure 14.2 illustrates this process.

FIGURE 14.2
A class diagram of
Calculator application

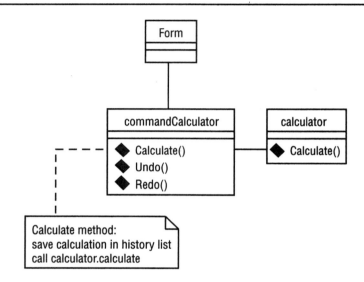

Here is the sample code for this application:

```
'************commandCalculator class************
'Declarations Section
  Dim rsHistory As New ADODB.Recordset
  Dim objCalc As New calculator

  Private Sub Class_Initialize()
  'create disconnected recordset
  With rsHistory.Fields
      .Append Name:="Operator", Type:=adChar, DefinedSize:=1
      .Append Name:="Num2", Type:=adDouble
      .Append Name:="Undone", Type:=adBoolean
  End With
  rsHistory.Open
  End Sub

  'function called by client that records calculation and passes request
to calculator
```

```
Public Function Calculate(Num1 As Double, Num2 As Double, Operator As _
String) As Double
  With rsHistory
      .AddNew
      .Fields("Operator").Value = Operator
      .Fields("Num2").Value = Num2
  End With
  Calculate = objCalc.Calculate(Num1, Num2, Operator)
  End Function


  'undoes the last calculation
  Public Function Undo(CurrentTotal As Double) As Double
  Dim Num2 As Double
  Dim sOperator As String
      With rsHistory
          'find any calculations that have not yet been undone
          .Filter = "Undone=False"
          If .EOF = False Then
              .MoveLast
              Num2 = .Fields("Num2")
              sOperator = .Fields("Operator")
              Select Case sOperator
              Case "-"
                  sOperator = "+"
              Case "+"
                  sOperator = "-"
              Case "/"
                  sOperator = "*"
              Case "*"
                  sOperator = "/"
              End Select
              Undo = objCalc.Calculate(CurrentTotal, Num2, sOperator)
  'mark calculations as undone
              .Fields("Undone") = True
          Else
              'no calculations to undo, CurrentTotal is unaffected
              Undo = CurrentTotal
          End If
      End With
  End Function
```

```
'redoes undone calculations
Public Function Redo(CurrentTotal As Double) As Double
Dim Num2 As Double
Dim sOperator As String
    With rsHistory
        'find any calculations that have been undone
        .Filter = "Undone=True"
        If .EOF = False Then
            .MoveLast
            Num2 = .Fields("Num2")
            sOperator = .Fields("Operator")
            Redo = objCalc.Calculate(CurrentTotal, Num2, sOperator)
            'mark calculations as not undone
            .Fields("Undone").Value = False
        Else
            'no calculations to redo CurrentTotal remains same
            Redo = CurrentTotal
        End If
    End With
End Function
'''''''''''''''''''''''''''


'**************calculator class****************

Public Function Calculate(Num1 as Double, Num2 as Double,Operator as
String)as Double
Select case Operator
Case "+"
Calculate = Num1 + Num2
Case "-"
Calculate = Num1 - Num2
Case "/"
Calculate = Num1 / Num2
Case "*"
Calculate = Num1 * Num2
End Select
End Function
'''''''''''''''''''''''''''
```

Other Uses of a Command Pattern

As mentioned, the command can save a request so that it can be executed at a later time. This is useful when the server object is not always available. The command can maintain a history list of all the times the request was called so that it can undo and redo actions as described in the sample command above. The command can also do preprocessing before actually executing the request. For example, if you want to add programmatic security checks on certain procedure calls, you can have the client call a command object that prompts the user for credentials before executing the request.

Related Patterns

The command pattern can be combined with several other patterns that take advantage of the flexibility of decoupling. These patterns include bridge, adapter, decorator, and facade. For example, if the client's request requires several procedure calls to multiple objects, the command object can double as a façade. In this case, the command provides one procedure for the client to call. That procedure takes on the status of an object, and in turn calls all the complex procedure calls to the server. Or if the server object's interface does not match what the client expects, then the command object can double as an adapter and provide a compatible interface for the client to call. Command then translates the call to match the server object's interface. You can also use the memento pattern to help command implement undo operations. Typically undo operations require the command object to record the state of the server object so that the server object can be properly restored when the undo function is called. Command can use the memento pattern to record, manage, and restore the server object's state.

NOTE   For more on related patterns, see Chapter 4, "The Bridge Pattern," Chapter 5, "The Adapter Pattern," Chapter 7, "The Decorator Pattern," Chapter 8, "The Facade Pattern," and Chapter 20, "The Memento Pattern."

Conclusion

The command pattern allows you to add intelligence and behavior to procedure calls without modifying the client or server. Of course you must modify the application so the client object points to the command object instead of the server. However, you don't have to add procedures and functionality to the client or the server because the command object acts an invisible intermediary. By turning the client procedure call into a smart object, command can assist in execution of the call, maintain the history or state of the call, or do preprocessing. Furthermore, since the command pattern completely decouples the client object from the server object, it can easily double as other patterns which also take advantage of decoupling.

chapter 15

The Interpreter Pattern

- A UML diagram of an interpreter pattern

- A sample use of an interpreter pattern

- Related patterns

The *interpreter* pattern is used to help an application understand a natural language statement and execute the intended functionality of the statement. Interpreter-type functionality is used every day by developers in the form of code compilers and utilities that execute SQL statements. There are many algorithms that can be used to provide this functionality; some algorithms provide good performance while others minimize resource consumption. The benefit of interpreter is the flexibility that it provides; it allows you to easily add new syntax rules and multiple implementations of a statement. To accomplish these tasks, interpreter goes through a four-step process. The interpreter:

1. Defines an abstract syntax

2. Parses the statement

3. Builds a programmatic representation of the statement in the form of an object model

4. Implements the intended functionality based upon the object model

First, the interpreter defines an abstract syntax so that the system can make sense of the natural language statement. An abstract syntax commonly has defined *clauses* that must follow a certain sequence, with each clause having a set of valid words. Consider SQL for a moment. A SQL SELECT statement begins with a SELECT clause followed by a FROM clause and optionally followed by a WHERE clause. The valid set of words for a SELECT clause are field names from the tables specified in the FROM clause. The valid set of words for the FROM clause are names of tables in the database.

Suppose we were defining abstract syntax for drawing simple graphics. The application allows users to draw or erase colored shapes with a natural language statement such as "Draw a red circle with a position of top=200, left=300." The first *clause*—draw a circle—would be the Action clause that has a value set of Draw or Erase. The next clause—red—would be Color and is optional. The next clauses would be Shape and Position. Shape can have a value set of the type of shapes the application can draw, and Position could be any numeric value.

The abstract syntax has a corresponding object model that reflects the structure and rules of the syntax. This object model is the programmatic representation of the statement. The clauses of the syntax can either be individual classes or properties of a class. For the graphical syntax we defined, the Action and Shape clauses can be classes, while the Color and Position clauses can be properties of the Color and Shape classes.

In the second stage of the interpreter pattern's four-step process, the interpreter parses the statement. The parser iterates through the clauses of the statement. In doing so, it instantiates and sets properties of the elements of the object model—properties which represent the intent of the statement. The object model reflects the rules and structure of the syntax, thus providing built-in syntax rules. The parser relies on these built-in rules to validate the syntax of the statement. The parser performs this validation while attempting to build the object model out of the statement. If a clause is missing or contains an invalid expression, then the object model will return an error. Because the parser iterates through the clauses and words of the statement, the parser can be responsible for some of the syntax rules, such as the sequence of the clauses or allowing certain literals. In parsing the natural language statement, then, the interpreter achieves step three of the process and builds a programmatic representation of the statement in the form of an object model.

Once the programmatic representation is complete, the system assesses the object model and implements the intended functionality in the final stage. You can use the visitor pattern to assess the object model. This would allow you to easily create multiple implementations of the statement.

NOTE   See Chapter 17 for more information on the visitor pattern.

A UML Diagram of an Interpreter Pattern

Figure 15.1 depicts the interpreter pattern, where the client passes a statement and passes a variable of typeExpression called objExpression to the parser's Parse method. The parser creates the expression object model based on the statement and stores it in the ByRef Expression parameter. After the Parse method runs, the client passes the object model stored in objExpression to StatementImplementer. In turn, StatementImplementer assesses the object model and implements the intended functionality. Figure 15.2 is a sequence diagram that depicts the steps taken in implementing the interpreter pattern.

```
ExpressionImplementer
```

Dim objExpression as Expression
Dim objImplementer as ExpressionImplementer

objParser.Parse(Statement,ByRef objExpression)
objImplementer.Build(objExpression)

Client

Parser

Expression

ClauseTypeA   ClauseTypeB

Client   Parser   Expression   ExpressionImplementer

Statement

Parse

Build Object Model

Return Object Model

Implement statement based on object model

A Sample Use of an Interpreter Pattern

For our sample, we'll use the graphic application example mentioned above. The application allows the user to enter an English-like command that directs the application to draw shapes on a form. The syntax definition consists of four clauses:

- An action clause that can be either Draw or Erase.

- A shape clause that can be either a box or circle.

- A color clause that can be either black, red, or blue.

- A position clause that can be top, left, height, or width. The position clause includes dimensions to keep things simple. The value set for any of these settings is any numeric value.

The syntax also allows for certain literals in the clauses so that the user can write English-like statements such as "draw a red box with a height of 200 and a width of 400" instead of "draw red circle height = 200, width = 400."

The application consists of a:

- Client form

- DrawShape class

- DrawAction

- Parser class

- VisitorForm class

Here is how the application works:

1. The user enters a statement into the textbox on the client form and clicks cmdExecute.

2. The form passes the statement to Parser.

3. Parser iterates through the statement, creates and sets properties of DrawAction and DrawShape. The parser validates the statement by checking whether the objects accepted the values. The parser is responsible for validating the sequence of clauses. The parser also knows when to ignore certain literals and not attempt to represent them in the object model.

4. If Parser encounters an invalid value, then it exits the procedure and returns an error string to the client.

5. When Parser is finished building DrawAction and DrawShape, it builds DrawStatement (DrawStatement includes DrawAction and DrawShape), and passes the DrawStatement object back to the client.

6. The form then passes DrawStatement and a reference to itself to VisitorForm.

7. VisitorForm draws the graphical interpretation of DrawStatement on the form that was passed to it.

In this example, DrawStatement, DrawAction, and DrawShape represent the abstract syntax for the application. DrawAction has one property called Action-Type, which can be set to either Draw or Erase. DrawShape has several properties that determine the characteristics of the shape to be drawn, such as ShapeType, Color, and so on. Each one of the properties has a valid set of possible values that is enforced either by the data type of the property or by code within the property let procedure.

The Parser class splits the statement into individual words and stores them in an array. The parser enumerates through the array, keeping track of which clause it is up to and sets the appropriate properties of DrawAction and DrawShape. Parser validates elements of the statement by checking if the object property has accepted the value.

When Parser is done, it adds DrawAction and DrawShape to DrawStatement and passes DrawStatement to the client form. The client form then passes Draw-Statement and itself to VisitorForm. VisitorForm uses Visual Basic's Shape control to draw shapes on the form. VisitorForm examines the objects and properties of DrawStatement, then sets the appropriate properties of the Shape control and adds it to the form.

Here is the code for DrawAction and DrawShape made up of properties that accept valid syntax values:

```
'*******************DrawAction Class*********************
'*******************Declarations Section
Public Enum ShapeAction
    shapeActionDraw
    shapeActionErase
End Enum
```

```
'***Valid values for ActionType
Const DRAW_ACTION = "draw"
Const ERASE_ACTION = "erase"
'***
Dim sShapeAction As String stores ActionType value
'*********************************************
Public Property Get ActionType() As String
ActionType = sShapeAction
End Property
'*********************************************
Public Property Let ActionType(ByVal Value As String)
Select Case LCase(Value)
Case LCase(DRAW_ACTION)
    sShapeAction = shapeActionDraw
Case LCase(ERASE_ACTION)
    sShapeAction = shapeActionErase
Case Else'if value is invalid then property is not set
    sShapeAction = ""
End Select
End Property


'******************DrawShape Class********************
'******************Declarations Section
Public Enum ShapeType
    shapeTypeSquare
    shapeTypeCircle
End Enum
'***Used to store value of properties
Dim nShapeType As Long
Dim nTop As Long
Dim nLeft As Long
Dim nHeight As Long
Dim nWidth As Long
Dim sShapeType As String
Dim sColor As String
Dim nColor As Long
'***Valid values for ShapeType and Color
Const SQUARE_SHAPE = "square"
Const BOX_SHAPE = "box"
Const CIRCLE_SHAPE = "circle"
Const LINE_SHAPE = "line"
Const COLOR_RED = "red"
```

```
Const COLOR_BLACK = "black"
Const COLOR_BLUE = "blue"

'*********************************************
Public Property Get TypeOfShape() As String
TypeOfShape = sShapeType
End Property
'*********************************************
Public Property Let TypeOfShape(ByVal Value As String)
Select Case LCase(Value)
Case BOX_SHAPE, SQUARE_SHAPE
    sShapeType = shapeTypeSquare
Case CIRCLE_SHAPE
    sShapeType = shapeTypeCircle
Case LINE_SHAPE
    sShapeType = shapeTypeLine
Case Else   'if value is invalid then property is not set
    sShapeType = ""
End Select
End Property
'*********************************************
Public Property Get Top() As Long
Top = nTop
End Property
'*********************************************
Public Property Let Top(ByVal Value As Long)
nTop = Value
End Property
'*********************************************
Public Property Get Left() As Long
Left = nLeft
End Property
'*********************************************
Public Property Let Left(ByVal Value As Long)
nLeft = Value
End Property
'*********************************************
Public Property Get Height() As Long
Height = nHeight
End Property
```

```
'********************************************
Public Property Let Height(ByVal Value As Long)
nHeight = Value
End Property
'********************************************
Public Property Get Width() As Long
Width = nWidth
End Property
'********************************************
Public Property Let Width(ByVal Value As Long)
nWidth = Value
End Property
'********************************************
Public Property Get Color() As String
Color = sColor
End Property
'********************************************
Public Property Let Color(ByVal Value As String)
sColor = Value
'***convert color to numeric value
Select Case Value
Case COLOR_BLACK
    nColor = vbBlack
Case COLOR_BLUE
    nColor = vbBlue
Case COLOR_RED
    nColor = vbRed
Case Else'value is invalid
    sColor = ""
End Select
End Property
'********************************************
'***numeric value of color so client can set Color properties to this
value
Public Property Get ColorNumber() As Long
ColorNumber = nColor
End Property
'********************************************
```

Here is the code for DrawStatement that serves simply to join DrawAction and DrawShape into a statement:

```
'*************DrawStatement Class*********************
'*************Declarations Section
Dim objShape As DrawShape
Dim objAction As DrawAction
'****************************************
Public Property Get Shape() As DrawShape
Set Shape = objShape
End Property
'****************************************
Public Property Set Shape(ByVal Value As DrawShape)
Set objShape = Value
End Property
'****************************************
Public Property Get Action() As DrawAction
Set Action = objAction
End Property
'****************************************
Public Property Set Action(ByVal Value As DrawAction)
Set objAction = Value
End Property
```

The following code for the Parser class iterates through the statement word by word and builds the DrawStatement object.

```
'***********Parser Class******************
'***********Declarations Section
Dim objStatement As DrawStatement
Dim objShape As DrawShape
Dim objAction As DrawAction
'***These values are ignored by the parser, which allows the statement
to be more english-like
Const A_LITERAL = "a"
Const TO_LITERAL = "to"
Const FROM_LITERAL = "from"
Const WITH_LITERAL = "with"
'***
```

```
'***This enum is used track the current clause that the parser is
dealing with
   Private Enum ParseStage
        stageAction
        stagecolor
        stageShape
        stagePosition
        stageSetPosition
        stageDone
   End Enum
   '***


   '*******************************************
   Public Function Parse(Statement As String, ByRef StatementObject As _
DrawStatement) As String
   Dim i As Integer'counter used to increment through the statement
   Dim vCommands As Variant'used to store the array returned by the Split
function on the statement
   Dim sMsg As String'error message
   Dim nStage As Integer'stores the current ParseStage
   Dim sPositionType As String
   Set objStatement = New DrawStatement
   Set objAction = New DrawAction
   Set objShape = New DrawShape
   '***replace all delimiters with spaces
   Statement = Replace(Statement, ",", " ")
   Statement = Replace(Statement, "=", " ")
   Statement = Replace(Statement, " of ", " ")
   '***
   '**break the statement into an array of individual words
   vCommands = Split(Statement, " ")
   '**
   i = 0
   smsg=""
   nStage = stageAction'first clause
   Do
        Select Case nStage
        Case stageAction
            objAction.ActionType = vCommands(i)
```

```
                '**validate the value by checking whether the property accepted the
value
            If objAction.ActionType = "" Then
                sMsg = vCommands(i) & " is not a valid action"
                Exit Do
            Else
    '**         'increment to the next word in the statement
                i = i + 1
                'move to the next clause
                nStage = stagecolor
            End If
        Case stagecolor
                '**allow the statement to be 'draw a circle'
            If vCommands(i) <> A_LITERAL Then
                objShape.Color = vCommands(i)
    '**color is optional so if value is not valid 'for color then don't
increment to the next word and use the current word for the shape
                If objShape.Color > "" Then
                    i = i + 1
                End If
                nStage = stageShape 'move to the next clause
            Else
    'word is ignored so remain in the same clause and move to the next word
                i = i + 1
            End If
        Case stageShape
            objShape.TypeOfShape = vCommands(i)
            If objShape.TypeOfShape = "" Then'validate
                sMsg = vCommands(i) & " is not a valid shape"
                Exit Do
            Else
    'move to the next word and clause
                i = i + 1
                nStage = stagePosition
            End If
        Case stagePosition
            Select Case LCase(vCommands(i))
            Case "top", "left", "height", "width"
                sPositionType = vCommands(i)
                nStage = stageSetPosition
            End Select
            i = i + 1
```

```
              Case stageSetPosition
                  If IsNumeric(Trim(vCommands(i))) = True Then
                      CallByName objShape, sPositionType, VbLet, _
CLng(vCommands(i))
                      i = i + 1
          'position is the last clause so remain in this 'clause until end of
statement
                      nStage = stagePosition
                  ElseIf Trim(vCommands(i)) = "" Then
                         'ignore spaces and move to next word
                      i = i + 1
                  Else
                      sMsg = vCommands(i) & " must be numeric"
                      Exit Do
                  End If
              End Select
          DoEvents
          Loop Until i = UBound(vCommands) + 1
          Set objStatement.Action = objAction
          Set objStatement.Shape = objShape
          Set StatementObject = objStatement
          Parse = sMsg
          End Function
```

The last class VisitorForm visits the DrawStatement object model and, using Visual Basic's Shape control, translates the properties into graphics:

```
'*************VisitorForm Class***************************
'****************************************
Public Function VisitShape(Statement As DrawStatement, Frm As Form) _
      As String
Dim sAction As String
Dim sShape As String
Dim objVBShape As VB.Shape
Static i As Integer
'**Insantiate instance of Shape control and add it to 'the form. The
name of the control is kept unique by 'incrementing the static I counter
in the next line 'of code
Set objVBShape = Frm.Controls.Add("vb.shape", "objShape" & i)
i = i + 1
'**
Select Case Statement.Shape.TypeOfShape
```

```
Case shapeTypeSquare
    objVBShape.Shape = vbShapeRectangle
Case shapeTypeCircle
    objVBShape.Shape = vbShapeCircle
End Select
With objVBShape
    .Left = Statement.Shape.Left
    .Top = Statement.Shape.Top
    .Height = Statement.Shape.Height
    .Width = Statement.Shape.Width
    Select Case Statement.Action.ActionType
    Case shapeActionDraw
        .BorderColor = Statement.Shape.ColorNumber
        .FillColor = Statement.Shape.ColorNumber
        .FillStyle = vbSolid
    Case shapeActionErase
        .BorderColor = Frm.BackColor
        .FillColor = Frm.BackColor
        .FillStyle = vbSolid
    End Select
    If Statement.Shape.Color > "" Then
    End If
    .ZOrder
    .Visible = True
End With
End Function
```

Related Patterns

In working with the interpreter pattern, you can also use several other patterns. First, you can use the composite pattern to build the syntax object model. Second, you can also use the iterator pattern to iterate through the object model. And third, you can use visitor to visit the object model and execute the intended functionality.

NOTE   Learn more about related patterns in Chapter 6, "The Composite Pattern," Chapter 16, "The Iterator Pattern," and Chapter 17, "The Visitor Pattern."

Conclusion

The interpreter pattern is an elegant way of translating English-like statements into intended functionality. Interpreter is best suited for simple syntaxes because complex syntaxes would require class hierarchies that are large and difficult to maintain in the form of an object model.

The Iterator Pattern

- Types of iterator patterns

- A UML diagram of an iterator pattern

- A sample use of an iterator pattern

- Other uses of an iterator

- Related patterns

The *iterator* pattern provides a method to sequentially access members of a collection. The iterator pattern separates the traversal mechanism and state management from an aggregate object. It removes the interface to traverse a group of objects from the aggregate object without revealing the underlying representation. Removing the mechanism to iterate through the collection allows you to use different algorithms to step through the collection—for example a forward iteration and a reverse iteration—without bloating the collection interface. In addition, the iterator pattern allows multiple clients to iterate through the same collection at different points. This is achieved because the iterator stores the state of the iteration. It is not in a collection, such as an ADO recordset, itself.

Types of Iterator Patterns

The iterator pattern is composed of an aggregate object along with an iterator object. The minimum interface that is implemented in the iterator object is FirstItem, NextItem, IsDone, and CurrentItem. More methods can be added to the iterator to create more complex objects. Some methods typically added are PreviousItem and LastItem to provide forward and reverse iteration.

Cursors

One determining factor that defines different types of iterator patterns is where the traversal algorithm is contained. In most implementations of the iterator patterns, the traversal algorithm is within the iterator object. However, the traversal algorithm could be implemented within the aggregate object. By removing this from the iterator, the iterator object is only left with storing the state of the traversal. The iterator remembers the point in the iteration. It remembers which step the traversal algorithm is in. This type of iterator object is called a *cursor*.

Robust Iterator

Another factor that creates different types of iterators is how *robust* an iterator is to changes in the aggregate. Adding and deleting elements in the aggregate can cause problems in the traversal algorithm. Iterators that can handle these types of changes in the aggregate are called *robust iterators*. A robust iterator is not affected by additions and deletions from the aggregate. A robust iterator traverses the aggregate as the aggregate is when the traversal starts. Objects added to the aggregate after the traversal begins will not be included within the traversal algorithm. In addition, objects deleted from the aggregate after the traversal begins will still be included within the traversal algorithm. This should be provided without having to copy the items within the aggregate.

Within VB, however, the For…Each construct is not robust. After the iteration has begun, the For…Each construct will include objects added to the collection and skip objects that have been deleted from the collection. Therefore, another mechanism is needed to remember which objects to traverse. The simplest method is to store a reference to the objects within the collection. This will allow deleted objects to be referenced, since the object would not be destroyed when the object is removed from the collection. This does not guard against changes made to the object.

Internal and External Iterators

The iterator pattern can also be separated into different types depending upon which object controls the iteration. In most cases, the client object will control the iteration. It will call the NextItem method and perform some action on the Current–Item. This type of iterator is called an *external iterator* .

The iteration can also be internalized to allow the iterator to control the traversal of the aggregate. In this scenario, the client passes a method to the iterator and it performs the method on each of the items in the aggregate. This can be implemented using the CallByName function. This type of iterator is called *an internal iterator*. The following is an example of an Iterate function of an internal iterator:

```
Private arrItems() as String

Public Sub Iterate(pObject As Object, pMethod As String)
    Dim i As Integer

    For i = 0 To UBound(arrItems) - 1
        CallByName pObject, pMethod, VbMethod, arrItems(i)
    Next
End Sub
```

The client object passes a reference to an object and the method to call for each item in a collection. The iterate method then calls this method for each item in the collection.

The one problem with implementing an internal iterator is that the methods passed to the iterate method must conform to some specific signature. In this example, the methods passed to the iterate method must only accept one string parameter. The advantage of the internal iterator is that the task of traversing the aggregate is internal to the iterator rather then the client.

A UML Diagram of an Iterator Pattern

The iterator pattern consists of two interfaces, IAggregate and IIterator along with concrete implementations of these interfaces. In the class diagram shown in Figure 16.1, the client asks the aggregate for an instance of the iterator object with the CreateIterator method. Internally, the iterator object stores a reference to the aggregate object.

FIGURE 16.1
A class diagram of an
iterator pattern

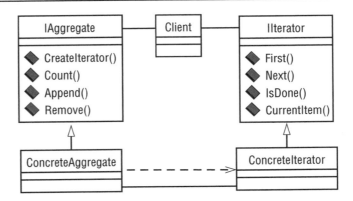

The aggregate object can be any collection of elements. In VB, the aggregate can be many different constructs. It may be a dictionary, array, collection, recordset, and so on. The iterator can be as simple as a wrapper around a recordset that stores the current position using a bookmark. Or it can be more complex by providing filtering or more complicated traversal algorithms than just forward and backward. The following demonstrates a simple implementation of the ConcreteIterator that wraps the functionality of the ADO recordset:

```
Private rs As ADODB.Recordset
Private varBookmark As Variant
Private bEof As Boolean
```

```
Public Sub MoveNext()
    rs.Bookmark = varBookmark
    rs.MoveNext
    varBookmark = rs.Bookmark
    bEof = rs.EOF
End Sub

Public Sub MoveLast()
    rs.MoveLast
    bEof = True
End Sub

Public Property Get IsDone () As Boolean
    IsDone = bEof
End Property

Public Property Get Recordset() As ADODB.Recordset
    Set Recordset = rs
End Property

Public Property Set Recordset(pRS As Recordset)
    Set rs = pRS
End Property
```

In ADO 2.5, the CurrentItem function could return the record object, instead of having to return the whole recordset.

A Sample Use of an Iterator Pattern

The iterator pattern is a natural fit for the VB collection object. The collection object can be used to implement the aggregate object and the iterator object can traverse the collection object. Figure 16.2 shows the class diagram of the sample application.

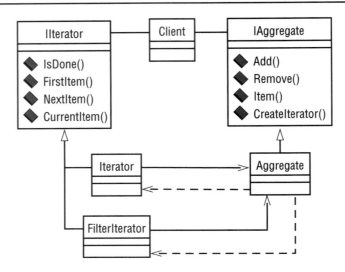

The sample has two iterators, a forward only iterator and a filter iterator. The forward only iterator allows a client to step through items within a collection, one after another. The filter iterator places a condition on the items so that only items that meet the criteria are returned to the client, while other items are passed over. Both of the iterators are robust external iterators. They both provide a mechanism to ignore additions to and deletions from the collection.

The sample contains two abstract interfaces, IIterator and IAggregate. IIterator contains the following interface:

```
' IIterator
Public Function IsDone() As Boolean
End Function

Public Sub FirstItem()
End Sub

Public Sub NextItem()
End Sub

Public Function CurrentItem() As Item
End Function

Public Sub Init(oAggregate As IAggregate)
End Sub
```

And IAggregate's interface is:

```
' IAggregate
Public Enum IteratorEnum
    ForwardIterator
    FilterIterator
End Enum

Public Sub Add(pItem As Item)
End Sub

Public Sub Remove(Key As String)
End Sub

Public Function Item(Index As Integer) As Item
End Function

Public Function Count() As Integer
End Function

Public Function CreateIterator(IteratorType _
    As IteratorEnum) As IIterator
End Function
```

The Aggregate class implements the IAggregate interface. It stores all of the items within the VB collection object and wraps the collection methods, Add, Remove, Item, and Count. In addition, the Aggregate class implements the Create-Iterator method. This method returns an instance of an iterator object initialized with a reference to the Aggregate object. The code for the CreateIterator method is the following:

```
Private Function IAggregate_CreateIterator(IteratorType _
    As IteratorEnum) As IIterator
    Dim oIterator As IIterator
    Select Case IteratorType
        Case FilterIterator
            Set oIterator = New FilterIterator
```

```
        Case ForwardIterator
            Set oIterator = New Iterator
    End Select

    oIterator.Init Me

    Set IAggregate_CreateIterator = oIterator
End Function
```

First the code instantiates an iterator object based on the IteratorType parameter and then it initializes the Iterator object using the Init method. The code for the Init method of the Iterator objects is the following:

```
Private Sub IIterator_Init(oAggregate As IAggregate)

    Dim j As Integer

    iCurrentItem = 1

    ReDim aItems(1 To oAggregate.Count)

    For j = 1 To oAggregate.Count
        Set aItems(j) = oAggregate.Item(j)
    Next
End Sub
```

The Init method stores a reference to all of the objects within the collection by placing them in an array. This allows the client to add and delete objects from the aggregate object without affecting the traversal of the object. It does not insulate the traversal algorithm from changes made to the item's properties. This is one method of making the iterator object robust.

The code behind the other methods within the Iterator class is the following:

```
Private oAggregate As IAggregate
Private aItems() As Item
Private iCurrentItem As Integer

Private Function IIterator_CurrentItem() As Item
    Set IIterator_CurrentItem = aItems(iCurrentItem)
End Function
```

```
Private Sub IIterator_FirstItem()
    iCurrentItem = 1
End Sub

Private Function IIterator_IsDone() As Boolean
    IIterator_IsDone = (UBound(aItems) < iCurrentItem)
End Function

Private Sub IIterator_NextItem()
    iCurrentItem = iCurrentItem + 1
End Sub
```

The state of the iteration is stored within iCurrentItem. Moving to the next item increases this variable and moving to the first item sets this variable to 1. The Current-Item is returned from the reference in the array. You can tell whether the traversal is done by comparing the upper bound of the array to the iCurrentItem variable.

The FilterIterator class implements the same code, except that the NextItem method tests the condition to ensure that the filter is met.

```
Private iCurrentItem as Integer

Private Sub FindNextFilterItem()
    Dim oItem As Item

    iCurrentItem = iCurrentItem + 1

    Do While iCurrentItem <= UBound(aItems)
        Set oItem = aItems(iCurrentItem)

        If oItem.Price < 1 Then Exit Do

        iCurrentItem = iCurrentItem + 1
    Loop
End Sub

Private Sub IIterator_FirstItem()
    iCurrentItem = 0
    FindNextFilterItem
End Sub
```

```
Private Sub IIterator_NextItem()
    FindNextFilterItem
End Sub

Private Sub Skip()
    While iCurrentItem <= Ubound(aItems) And _
        aItems(iCurrentItem).Price < 1

        iCurrentItem = iCurrentItem + 1
    Wend
End Sub

Private Sub IIterator_FirstItem()
    iCurrentItem = 1
    Skip
End Sub

Private Sub IIterator_NextItem()
    iCurrentItem = iCurrentItem + 1
    Skip
End Sub
```

The NextItem method iterates to the next item and then scans ahead to see if there are any other items that meet the criteria. The criterion, in this case, is that the price has to be greater than or equal to one dollar.

The client code that controls the iteration is shown below:

```
Private Sub cmdIterate_Click()
    Dim oIterator As IIterator
    Dim oItem As Item

    Set oIterator = _
    oAggregate.CreateIterator(FilterIterator)

    oIterator.FirstItem

    Do While Not oIterator.IsDone
        Set oItem = oIterator.CurrentItem
        MsgBox oItem.Name
        oIterator.NextItem
    Loop
End Sub
```

The code just iterates through the collection and displays the name of each item in a message box.

Other Uses of an Iterator

The iterator pattern can be used with any aggregate object to separate the traversal mechanism from the aggregate object. In addition to traversing simple one-dimensional collections, the iterator pattern can be used to traverse more complicated structures, like composites and hierarchies. In this scenario, the iterator would traverse each object along with its children in a recursive manner. For example, one hierarchy that might be iterated through is the organizational chart of a company. Figure 16.3 shows part of a company called XYZ. The iterator for this hierarchy would begin with the Company and move through each node of the chart.

FIGURE 16.3

Iterators can traverse complicated multi-dimensional hierarchies like an organization chart

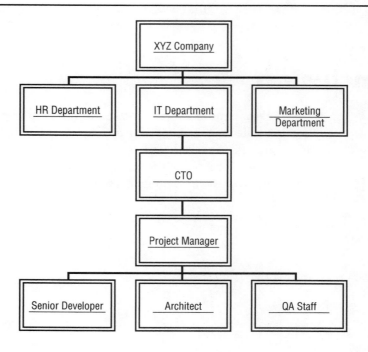

Related Patterns

Iterators are often used to traverse composites. In so doing, the iterator must be able to recursively traverse the hierarchical structure of the composite.

The memento pattern is often used with the iterator to store the state of the iteration. Implemented within the iterator object, the memento can remember at what point in the traversal the iterator is in.

NOTE   Learn more about related patterns in Chapter 6, "The Composite Pattern," and Chapter 20, "The Memento Pattern."

Conclusion

The iterator pattern is a powerful pattern used to separate the traversal algorithm and the state management from an aggregate object. By moving these two parts of the aggregate to a new object, you can implement multiple traversal algorithms on objects without bloating the interface. In addition, multiple traversals can occur simultaneously on an aggregate object.

The Visitor Pattern

- Implementing visitor

- A UML diagram of a visitor pattern

- An example of a visitor pattern

- Sample code for a visitor pattern

- Related patterns

Y ou can use the *visitor* pattern when operations must be performed upon numerous elements of an object model. Without the visitor, this type of functionality is usually implemented by spreading the required operations throughout the object model. Visitor provides a cleaner and more flexible model by abstracting the operations from the elements of the object model, and turning them into visitor objects. The visitor objects traverse the object model and perform their respective operations upon the individual elements. A useful way of viewing visitor is by looking at the object model as the representation of a state and the visitor as agents that act upon the state. Abstracting the operations from the object model into visitor objects benefits you by allowing you to:

- Easily add or remove operations without modifying the elements of the object model.

- Group together related functions that may otherwise have to be spread throughout the object model.

Implementing Visitor

There are several issues to consider when implementing visitor, including:

- Allowing a visitor to visit objects with differing interfaces

- Determining who is responsible for traversing the object model

- Accumulating and sharing state

Allowing a Visitor to Visit Objects with Differing Interfaces

In many cases, a visitor will have to visit multiple classes in an object model; and these classes have a number of different interfaces. So although the visitor may be performing the same operation on all the objects, it still needs to address each object differently. To solve this problem the visitor generally has a separate visit method for each type of class it has to access. Each individual visitor method recognizes its targeted class and is able to access it accordingly.

Traversing the Object Model

When a visitor has to visit multiple objects in an object model, there are several ways it can traverse the object model:

- The client can iterate through the model and pass each object to its appropriate visitor.

- The visitor itself can be provided with understanding of the model and traverse the model by itself.

- A separate iterator object can traverse the model and pass each object to its appropriate visitor.

If you choose to have the client or an iterator object traverse the model, then the client or iterator will have to match each element of the model to its visitor and call the appropriate visit method of the visitor. If you want to have a thin client or iterator that doesn't have to know the individual methods of the visitor, then you can define an accept method for each element in the object model. The accept method accepts a visitor as a parameter and calls the appropriate method of the visitor. This method is depicted in Figure 17.2 in the next section, "A UML Diagram of a Visitor Pattern."

Accumulating and Sharing States

In some cases a visitor may need to retain the state of the objects it visits—for example, a visitor that calculates a sum total based on the properties of the objects it visits. The visitor has to store the state across visits and has to make the state available to the object that requires it.

A UML Diagram of a Visitor Pattern

Figure 17.1 depicts a visitor that was implemented by having a client iterate through the elements of an object model. For each element, the client calls the appropriate method of the visitor and passes the element as a parameter.

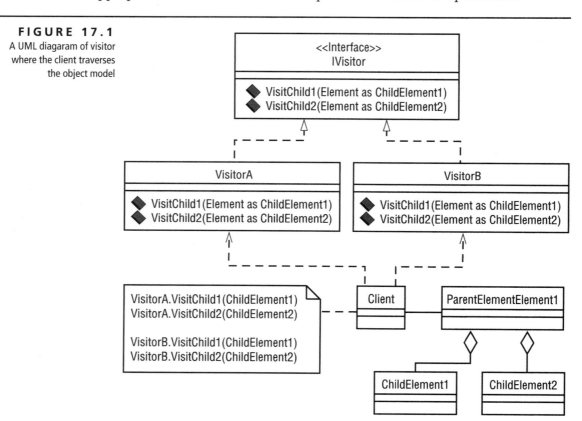

Figure 17.2 depicts a visitor where the client doesn't have to know the methods of the visitor. It simply passes the appropriate visitor object to the elements and the elements call the appropriate methods.

FIGURE 17.2

A UML diagram of a visitor where the client traverses the object model, but the elements of the model are responsible for calling the appropriate methods of the visitor

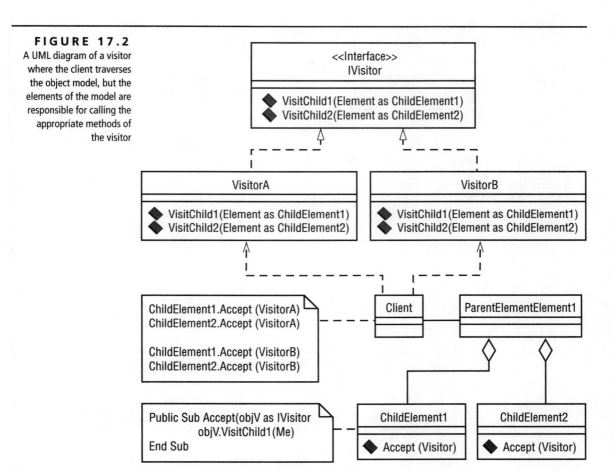

An Example of a Visitor Pattern

For our sample visitor, we'll use a timesheet application that calculates the time and reimbursements of employees. The functionality and rules for the application are as follows. Employees report specific expenses, as well as their work hours, which are identified by corresponding codes. The reimbursements for the individual codes vary depending on the position of each employee. The timesheet application must also keep track of the company's employee motivation plan. Through this plan, employees receive bonus points for keeping their expenses low and for time codes deemed especially valuable to the company. The system must be flexible enough to allow for new motivation plans to be easily implemented.

The object model for the application is made up of a top-level class called Timesheet. The time and expense related line items are represented in the object model as TimeItem and ExpItem, respectively. The application has two visitor objects, VisitorReimb and VisitorBonus. VisitorReimb visits both TimeItems and ExpItems and calculates the total reimbursements for the timesheet. VisitorBonus is an implementation of IVisitorBonus. VisitorBonus visits both TimeItems and ExpItems and calculates the bonus points for a particular motivation plan. Figure 17.3 shows the object model for this application and Figure 17.4 depicts the interactions between the objects in a sequence diagram.

FIGURE 17.3
An object model for the
Timesheet application

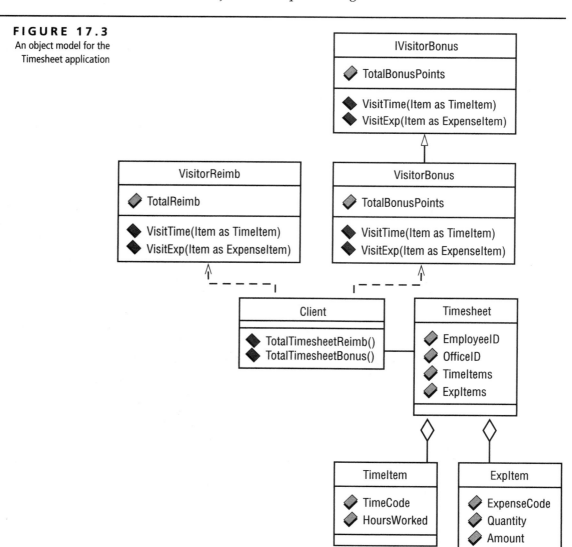

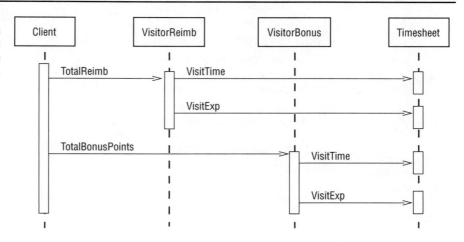

FIGURE 17.4
A sequence diagram showing the collaborations and interactions of the Timesheet application

Sample Code for a Visitor Pattern

For this sample, the client will iterate through the object model and pass the individual elements to the visitor objects. Here's the code for the application that performs the visitor functionality:

```
'*********************Client Form*********************
'*********************Declarations Section
Dim objTimeSheet as New TimeSheet


'********Function that returns total reimbursement for a
'timesheet
Public Function TotalTimeSheetReimb() As Single
Dim objVReimb as New VisitorReimb
Dim objTime as TimeItem
Dim objExp as ExpItem
Dim sngTotalReimb as Single
'*****Calculate Reimbursement for time and expenses
With objTimesheet
'**Reimbursement for time
```

```
    For Each objTime In .TimeItems
        ObjVReimb.VisitTime objTime
    Next ObjTime
    SngReimb = ObjVReimb.TotalReimb
    '**Reimbursement for expenses
    For Each objExp In .ExpItems
        objVReimb.VisitExp objExp
    Next ObjExp
    sngReimb = sngReimb + objVReimb.TotalReimb
    End With
    TotalTimeSheetReimb=sngReimb
    End Function


    '******Function that returns total bonus points for a
'timesheet***********
    Public Function TotalTimeSheetBonus() As Single
    Dim objVBonus as IVisitorBonus
    Dim objTime as TimeItem
    Dim objExp as ExpItem
    Dim sngTotalBonus as Single
    '**objVBonus is typed as Ivisitor which is an abstract 'interface so it
'has to be set to instance of an 'implementstion of the interface
    Set objVBonus = New VisitorBonus
    '*****Calculate bonus points for time and expenses
    With objTimesheet
    '**Bonus for time
    For Each objTime In .TimeItems
        ObjVBonus.VisitTime objTime
    Next ObjTime
    sngTotalBonus = ObjVBonus.TotalBonusPoints
    '**Bonus for expenses
    For Each objExp In .ExpItems
        objVBonus.VisitExp objExp
    Next ObjExp
    sngTotalBonus = sngTotalBonus + _ objVBonus.TotalBonusPoints
    End With
    TotalTimeSheetBonus = sngTotalBonus
    End Function
```

If the company wants to add a new motivation plan then we can create a new implementation of IVisitorBonus and call it in the TotalTimesheetBonus function of the client, as follows:

```
'******Function that returns total bonus points for a
'timesheet***********
  Public Function TotalTimeSheetBonus() As Single
  Dim objVBonus as IVisitorBonus
  Dim objVBonus2 as IVisitorBonus
  Dim objTime as TimeItem
  Dim objExp as ExpItem
  Dim sngTotalBonus as Single
  '**objVBonus and objVBonus2 are typed as Ivisitor which is an abstract
'interface so they have to be set to 'instance of an implementation of the
'interface
  Set objVBonus = New VisitorBonus
  '*****Calculate bonus points for time and expenses
  With objTimesheet
  '**Bonus for time
  For Each objTime In .TimeItems
      objVBonus.VisitTime objTime
      objVBonus2.VisitTime objTime
  Next objTime
  sngTotalBonus =ObjVBonus.TotalBonusPoints + _
      ObjVBonus2.TotalBonusPoints
  '**Bonus for expenses
  For Each objExp In .ExpItems
      objVBonus.VisitExp objExp
      objVBonus2.VisitExp objExp
  Next objExp
  sngTotalBonus = sngTotalBonus + objVBonus.TotalBonusPoints +  _
   ObjVBonus2.TotalBonusPoints
  End With
  TotalTimeSheetBonus = sngTotalBonus
  End Function
```

Related Patterns

Composite, which is essentially an object model, is an ideal candidate for the visitor pattern. Iterator is commonly used in conjunction with visitor to iterate through the elements of the object model that visitor is targeting.

NOTE   To learn more about related patterns, see Chapter 6, "The Composite Pattern," and Chapter 16, "The Iterator Pattern."

Conclusion

The visitor pattern allows you to keep an object model neat by abstracting the operations that have to be performed on the elements of the model into separate objects. It also allows you to easily add or remove operations without touching the elements of the model. Use visitor when you either have an extensive object model or want to provide the flexibility of modifying the operations.

chapter 18

The Template Method Pattern

- Types of templates

- A UML diagram of a template method pattern

- A sample use of a template method pattern

- Sample code for a template method

- Related patterns

The *template method* pattern is a simple, yet fundamental pattern for code reuse. It helps you avoid spaghetti code by standardizing the steps of the code first and then implementing each individual step. This method allows new developers to easily understand the steps in a given process, by separating the list of steps from the actions taken in each particular step.

The key to this pattern is putting the skeleton of an algorithm within a method (the template method). Steps in the algorithm become methods called from the template method. This keeps the overall algorithm constant, while allowing you to change how the individual steps of the algorithm are carried out. Let's say you are writing a data conversion routine that has the following steps:

1. Open connections to source and target databases.

2. Truncate the tables in the target database.

3. Fill target database tables.

4. Close connections.

Using the template method pattern, you can construct the outline of this algorithm in the following manner:

```
Public Function Convert()
    OpenConnections
    TruncateTables
    FillTables
    CloseConnections
End Function
```

In this way, the template method pattern organizes code effectively.

Types of Templates

In addition to being a neat way of organizing code, the template pattern also gives you a lot of flexibility. It does so by allowing you to create a standard template method for a general problem domain and then customize it to solve particular instances of the problem. You customize it by changing the way individual steps of the algorithm are implemented.

In languages that support inheritance, you achieve customization through sub-classing the template class. In Visual Basic 6.0, which does not support inheritance, you can achieve customization through object composition in the following manner. The template method is implemented in a class called Template. However, the operations of the template method that may need to be customized are implemented in a separate class that we will call CustomTemplate. Clients of the template class are responsible for supplying an implementation of CustomTemplate class to Template. Clients can then customize the implementation of the methods in CustomTemplate to suit their needs. They can then pass a reference of Custom-Template to the template method through a property of the template class. In turn, the template class will use the CustomTemplate passed by the client to carry out the operations in the template method.

The template method pattern breaks down the methods (operations) that are called from the template method into four categories.

Abstract Operations   Also called *primitive operations,* you use abstract operations for functionality that varies from case to case. In languages that support inheritance, abstract operations are methods that are empty in the abstract class but *must* be filled-in in the subclasses. In Visual Basic, these types of operations are part of the CustomTemplate interface and must be implemented by the client.

Concrete Operations   Concrete operations are used for operations that don't vary from case to case. They are therefore implemented in the template class. In languages that support inheritance, subclasses can override the default behavior of the superclass. Therefore such languages can also use concrete operations for functionality that has a default behavior but may vary from case to case.

Factory Methods   Factory methods are methods that create an object. Typically a factory method creates a default object type, but also allows clients to specify via a parameter the type of object to create.

Hook Operations   You use hook operations as places to put code where the developer predicts that future flexibility will be required. Three of the keys to placement of hook operations in a template method are "location, location, location." To implement hook operations successfully, the developer must foresee where the need for flexibility will be required in the future. In languages that support inheritance, hooks are empty methods that can be optionally filled in by subclasses. In object composition, hook operations are part of the abstract interface and are implemented by the client just like abstract operations. The difference between abstract and hook is conceptual and can generally be seen in their names. Abstract operations have a specific purpose and have names that describe that purpose, like ImportFile or CheckValidity, while hooks are placeholders and usually have names like Preprocess and Postprocess.

A UML Diagram of a Template Method Pattern

Figure 18.1 depicts a template pattern that uses object composition to allow clients to customize the implementation of the template method. The ICustomTemplate interface defines the methods that must be implemented by the client and will be called by the template method. OperationA is a concrete operation implemented by Template and therefore cannot be changed by clients. OperationHook is a placeholder for clients to implement any functionality that has to be executed before any other methods are called.

```
Private objCustom as ICustomTemplate
Public Property Set CustomTemplate(objTemplate As _ ICustomTemplate)

    Set objCustom = objTemplate

End Property

Public Sub Execute()
   OperationHook
   OperationA
   With objCustom
      .Operation1
      .Operation2
   End With
End Sub
```

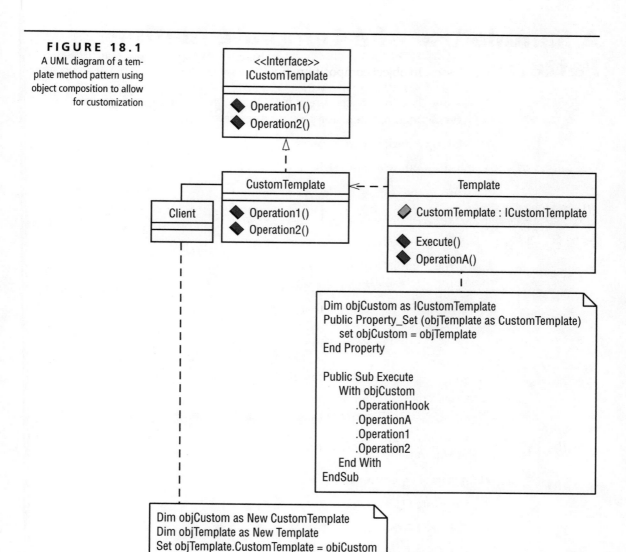

A Sample Use of a Template Method Pattern

Let's assume that you are creating a class that is the basis for card games. Use cases have defined the steps for playing most card games:

1. Making a deck of card objects
2. Shuffling the deck of cards
3. Cutting the deck of cards
4. Dealing the cards
5. Playing the game

Using the Template Method pattern, you can construct the outline of the algorithm above in the StartGame method of the Game class:

```
Public Function StartGame()
    CreateDeck
    ShuffleDeck
    CutDeck
    DealCards
    Play
End Function
```

In the above code, the StartGame method is the template method. The individual operations of the StartGame method can be classified in the four categories of template operations:

- Abstract Operations
- Concrete Operations
- Factory Methods
- Hook Operations

The DealCards and Play methods are examples of an abstract operation. These methods of a Poker subclass of AbstractGame would be different from the Play method of a Solitaire subclass of AbstractGame. There is no default behavior for these methods because every game is played differently. Therefore, these two must be defined in the subclass. Using object composition in Visual Basic, these two would be operations implemented in CustomTemplate.

The CutDeck and ShuffleDeck methods are examples of concrete operations. Once the Deck has been created, cutting and shuffling a deck are the same in most card games. Filling in the cutting and shuffling methods in the abstract class provides all subclasses with a default behavior common to most card games. The game creator does not even have to think about it; the template class automatically knows how to cut and shuffle its deck. Languages that support inheritance can accommodate the five percent of games that cut or shuffle a deck differently by allowing the subclass to override these methods.

The CreateDeck method is an example of a factory method. The default deck type created by this method could be a Deck object that contains a standard set of Playing Card objects. Any clients that use a different type of Deck can instantiate the desired type of Deck object in the CreateDeck method. The card game Concentration would create a Deck object that contained card objects with all sorts of designs and pictures, rather than the standard deck of playing cards. In Visual Basic you would implement this by having the CreateDeck have an optional parameter that specifies which type of deck to create. If you do not want to limit clients to a finite set of decks then you would have to move away from the factory concept that shields the client from knowing how to create the objects. You would have to use object composition by defining an abstract interface for the Deck object. The client would have to implement the interface, customize it, instantiate it, and pass it to the CreateDeck method.

When performing use cases for card games, secondary use cases show that most of the variation in the steps in the algorithm occurs around the dealing of cards. For instance, in the game of poker, the players ante up before the cards are dealt, and bet money after the cards are dealt. In one version of Poker, after cards are dealt, players each pass a card to the player next to them. To provide hooks for handling these secondary cases, hook operations (BeforeDealCards and After-DealCards) can be placed around the DealCards method. The following code depicts these hooks:

```
Public Function StartGame()
   CreateDeck
   CutDeck
```

```
        ShuffleDeck
        BeforeDealCards
        DealCards
        AfterDealCards
        Play
End Function
```

Using object implementation to implement these hook operations—BeforeDeal-Cards and AfterDealCards—you would use five classes as shown in Figure 18.2.

Game   This class contains the template method StartGame, the concrete operations CreateDeck, CutDeck, and the factory method CreateDeck.

ICustomGame   This abstract interface contains the procedure declarations for the abstract operations of DealCards and Play. It also contains the hook operations BeforeDealCards and AfterDealCards, as well as a read-only property called Deck. The template method reads the Deck property to determine which kind of deck to create with the CreateDeck method.

PokerGame   This class implements ICustomGame and contains custom code for abstract and hook operations. It also sets the value of the Deck property.

Deck   This class is created by the CreateDeck method. It will not be shown in the sample code because it isn't pertinent to the template pattern aspect of the example.

Client   This class chooses the type of custom game by instantiating the PokerGame class. It then instantiates the Game class and sets Game's CustomGame property to the instance of PokerGame. It then starts the game by calling Game's StartGame method.

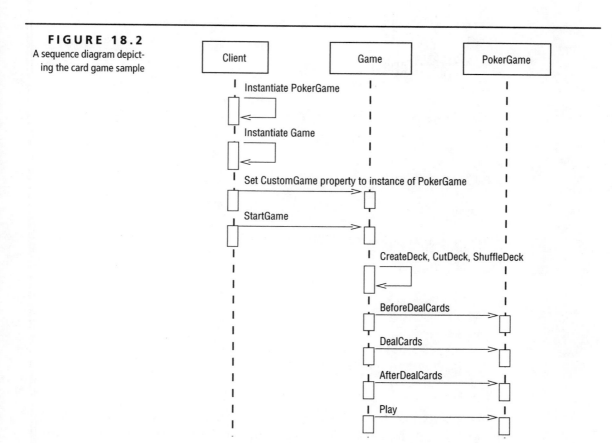

FIGURE 18.2
A sequence diagram depicting the card game sample

Sample Code for the Template Method Pattern

The code below shows the ICustomGame abstract class, the PokerGame class, Game class and client code for a sample poker game.

The ICustomGame Abstract class simply defines our interface for a custom game.

```vb
'*****************ICustomGame Abstract Class**********
Public Enum DeckType
    deckStandard
    deckConcentration
End Enum

Public Sub BeforeDealCards()

End Sub

Public Sub DealCards()

End Sub

Public Sub AfterDealCards()

End Sub

Public Sub Play()

End Sub

Public Property Get Deck() As DeckType

End Property
```

The PokerGame class uses the interface provided by ICustomGame and fills in the specific code for a poker game—particularly the approach for dealing cards, what type of deck to use, and how the game is played.

```vb
'*****************PokerGame Class***************
Implements ICustomGame

Private Sub ICustomGame_BeforeDealCards()
'prehook operation
'custom code for ante up before cards are dealt
End Sub

Private Sub ICustomGame_AfterDealCards()
'posthook operation
'custom code for betting after cards are dealt
End Sub
```

```
Private Sub ICustomGame_DealCards()
'custom code for dealing cards for poker game
End Sub

Private Property Get ICustomGame_Deck() As DeckType
    ICustomGame_Deck = deckStandard
End Property

Private Sub ICustomGame_Play()
'custom code for playing poker game
End Sub
```

The Game class also uses the interface provided by ICustomGame in order to specify how the deck is created, the order in which things occur (this is our template method, StartGame), and how to cut and shuffle the deck.

```
'*********************Game Class**************
Dim objCustomGame As ICustomGame

Public Function StartGame()        'template method
    CreatDeck objCustomGame.Deck    'concrete operation
    CutDeck                         'concrete operation
    ShuffleDeck                     'concrete operation
        With objCustomGame
            .BeforeDealCards    'hook operation
            .DealCards          'abstract operation
            .AfterDealCards     'hook operation
            .Play               'abstract operation
        End With
End Function

Private Sub CreatDeck(TypeOfDeck As DeckType)
    'code that creates deck
End Sub

Private Sub CutDeck()
    'code that cuts deck
End Sub

Private Sub ShuffleDeck()
    'code that shuffles deck
End Sub
```

```
Public Property Set CustomGame(CustomGameObject As ICustomGame)
    Set objCustomGame = CustomGameObject
End Property
```

Finally, our client class shows how easy it is to start a poker game. We simply create a new PokerGame object, and then start the game.

```
'********************Client Class*****************
Dim objGame As New Game
Dim objPoker As ICustomGame 'declare as interface type

Public Sub PlayGame()
'instantiate custom game
    Set objPoker = New PokerGame
    'pass Game a reference to custom class
    Set objGame.CustomGame = objPoker
    objGame.StartGame
End Sub
```

Related Patterns

The template method pattern is commonly used with the hook and factory patterns. Within the template method, the hook pattern is used to provide placeholders for developers to add currently undefined code. Serving a different function, the factory pattern is used in the template when objects have to be created as part of the template algorithm.

NOTE Learn more about related patterns in Chapter 19, "The Hook Pattern," and Chapter 23, "The Factory Pattern."

Conclusion

The template method pattern is best suited for when you are implementing a defined algorithm. It helps you avoid spaghetti code by standardizing the steps of the code first and then implementing each individual step. You will enjoy two particular benefits from using the template method pattern. First, moving from use case to class design is simpler. Notice how the use case steps each become a method. Second, if done correctly, a template method can be self-documenting. A developer who is new to the game project should have no problem understanding the StartGame method. In addition to being an organization tool, the template method can be used with inheritance or object composition to provide the flexibility to solve many instances of a given problem.

chapter 19

The Hook Pattern

- Location and parameters of hook patterns

- A UML diagram of a hook pattern

- A sample use of a hook pattern

- Related patterns

Hook is a simple, flexible pattern that developers can use to allow future developers to implement currently unforeseen functionality. A hook is simply a call from within a working routine to an unimplemented procedure. (An unimplemented procedure consists of only the procedure stub without any implementation code.) The call to the procedure is known as the *hook operation*, and the empty procedure is known as the *hook*. In the future, developers write the code for unforeseen functionality in the hook procedure.

Visual Basic developers take advantage of hooks all the time in the form of events. Many objects raise events before or after significant actions take place, to allow clients to implement some additional functionality. The object that raises the event contains the hook operation in the form of a RaiseEvent method. The client contains the hook procedure in the form of an Event procedure stub in which code can be added. The ADO recordset object, for example, is chock-full of hooks. It has events before and after almost all actions it performs, including WillMove, MoveComplete, WillChangeField, FiledChangeComplete, and other actions.

Location and Parameters of Hook Patterns

There are several issues to consider when implementing hooks, including where to place the hook procedure, where to place the hook operation, and what information should be passed to a hook procedure.

Location of the Hook Operation

The value of a hook is wholly dependent on where it is placed. The hook operation is commonly placed either before a critical process begins or after a critical process is over. By placing the hook before the critical process begins, you allow the developer working with the object to abort the process or to perform preprocessing. This type of hook is known as a *preprocessor hook*. An example of a preprocessor hook in Visual Basic is the Unload event of a form. The event is raised before the process of unloading begins. As a result, the developer working on the form has the opportunity to implement custom functionality. For example, by setting the event's cancel parameter to true, the application can prompt the user to save data on the form before unloading or aborting the unload process.

In contrast, by placing the hook after the process occurs, you allow the developer to do some cleanup. This type of hook is known as a *postprocessor hook*. In Visual Basic, an example of a postprocessor hook is the Terminate event of a form.

This event is raised after the form is unloaded and allows the developer to perform cleanup after the form unloads.

Location of the Hook Procedure

The decision about where to place the hook procedure is dependent upon who will add the functionality later. As described above, a hook operation calls out to a hook procedure. The hook procedure is where functionality can be added in the future. The hook procedure can be implemented in multiple locations:

1. In a procedure within the same module that has the hook operation. This is the simplest approach. It is simply a call from one procedure to an empty procedure within the same class or in a standard module. Choose this method if the future functionality will be implemented by somebody who can modify the source code of your object.

2. In the client of the object that makes the hook call. This approach is implemented as an event that is raised from the object to the client. Choose this method if you want the clients of the object to be able to add functionality that will vary from client to client.

3. In an external object. To implement this, have the hook call out to empty methods of an object with a defined interface. The object containing the hook operation should have a public property that allows clients to point to an instance of a concrete hook object. Choose this method over the event-driven method if you intend for the object to be extended to include standard functionality that will not be changed from client to client.

Hook Parameters

To ensure that a hook provides value, it must pass sufficient information to the hook procedure to allow the hook procedure to perform some useful functionality. For example, a preprocessor hook may pass information about its current state and how the process that is about to begin will affect it. A postprocessor hook may pass information about the new state or about whether the process was successful. The ADO recordset's WillChangeFiled and FieldChangeComplete events are preprocessor and postprocessor hooks, respectively. Both of their parameters provide information about which fields are affected by the change, the new values of the fields, and why they are changing. In addition, FieldChangeComplete provides information about the success of the operation. There obviously is no set rule on whether to pass information to a hook procedure or what information to pass. Each case has to be analyzed to determine what information, if any, would be of value to the developer who will implement the hook procedure.

A UML Diagram of a Hook Pattern

Figure 19.1 depicts simple pre- and postprocedural hooks, where a working procedure calls to an empty procedure that is destined to be filled in at a later date.

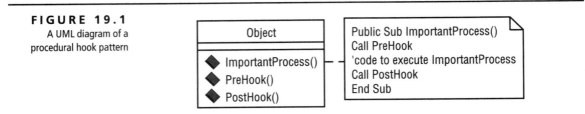

Figure 19.2 depicts a server object that implements a preprocessor hook in the form of an event. Note that the Cancel parameter of the event allows the client to abort the process.

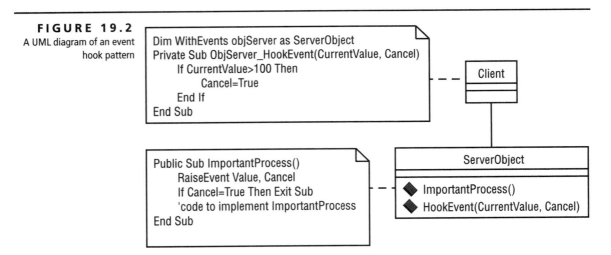

Figure 19.3 depicts an object hook where the server object performs a hook operation by calling to the Execute procedure of an external hook object. The client provides the external hook object so that it can implement the hook procedure. In order for the client and server objects to work together, an abstract interface is defined for the hook object. A developer customizes the concrete hook class to suit his or her needs. Once the developer has created the concrete hook class, the client object creates an instance of the concrete hook and sets the server object's

HookObject property to reference it. The server object calls to the concrete hook object before it begins executing ImportantProcess. Figure 19.4 depicts this same flow of events in a sequence diagram.

FIGURE 19.3
A UML diagram of an
object hook pattern

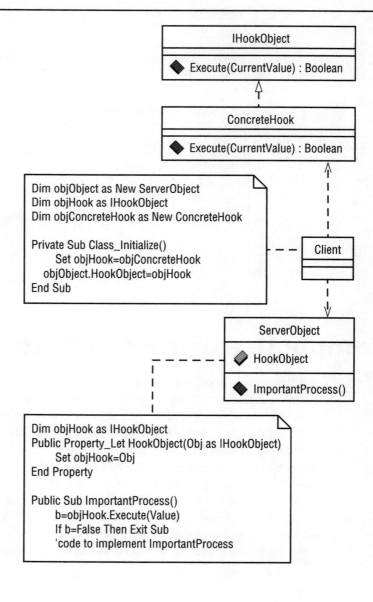

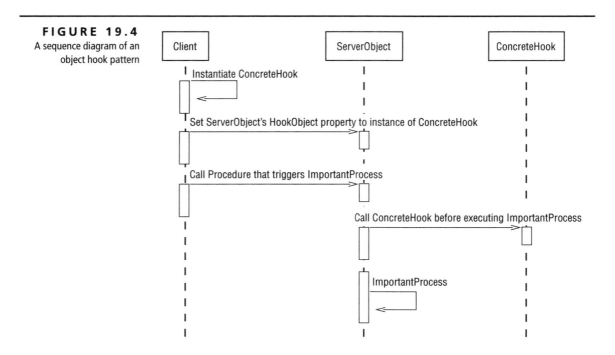

FIGURE 19.4
A sequence diagram of an object hook pattern

A Sample Use of a Hook Pattern
==

For the sample hook, we'll look at implementing pre- and postprocessor hooks using events. Here's the scenario: You are developing an object that converts RTF files to HTML files. It will be the standard converter used by all developers in your organization. Since it will be used in many different projects, there is no way you can anticipate all the varying functionality it will need. For some projects, users will want to preprocess the text before it is converted. For other projects, you will want to allow the user to review and edit the converted text before it is saved to file. To work around this problem, you can use preprocessor and postprocessor hooks. Before the conversion, raise an event called WillConvert that passes the RTF as a ByRef parameter. In this way, the client can change the text. After the text is converted, pass the text as a ByRef parameter to an event called ConvertComplete.

These hooks will allow each instance of the HTMLConverter class to be extended to include custom pre- and postprocessing. Here's the code:

```
'***************** HTMLConverter Class*************
'Declarations
Public Event WillConvert(ByRef Text As String)
Public Event ConvertComplete(ByRef Text As String)

Public Function ConvertFile(SourceFile As String, _ DestinationFile As
String)
    Dim sText As String
    Dim fso As New FileSystemObject
    Dim txtStream As TextStream

    'open and read source
    Set txtStream = fso.OpenTextFile(SourceFile)
    sText = txtStream.ReadAll

    'preprocessor hook
    RaiseEvent WillConvert(sText)

    'procedure that parses and tags text
    sText = Convert(sText)

    'postprocessor hook
    RaiseEvent ConvertComplete(sText)

    'write text to file
    Set txtStream = fso.CreateTextFile(DestinationFile)
    txtStream.Write sText
End Function

'****************** Client Form*************
'Declarations
Dim WithEvents objHTML As HTMLConverter

Private Sub cmdConvert_Click()
    objHTML.ConvertFile "D:\Source.rtf", "Destination.htm"
End Sub

Private Sub Form_Load()
    Set objHTML = New HTMLConverter
End Sub
```

```
'preprocessor hook procedure
Private Sub objHTML_ConvertComplete(Text As String)
    'custom preprocessing goes here
End Sub

'postprocessor hook procedure
Private Sub objHTML_WillConvert(Text As String)
    'custom postprocessing goes here
End Sub
```

Related Patterns

The hook pattern is commonly used in conjunction with two other patterns, template and factory. The template pattern defines the steps for an algorithm. Hook operations can be placed at strategic intervals in the algorithm to allow a developer to add currently undefined steps to the algorithm.

The factory pattern is used to create a group of related objects called products. Hooks are commonly used within the factory pattern to allow the factory to create extended versions of products.

> **NOTE**   Learn more about the template method pattern in Chapter 18 and the factory pattern in Chapter 23.

Conclusion

All patterns, in one way or another, aim to make software systems more flexible. Hook goes beyond that and makes a system extensible by giving developers the opportunity to hook in currently undefined functionality. Using event hooks, you can allow for each instance of your object to be extended to include unique functionality. Object hooks, on the other hand, allow developers to add standard functionality to an object that clients cannot change.

chapter 20

The Memento Pattern

- Understanding memento's design

- A UML diagram of a memento pattern

- A sample use of a memento pattern

- Related patterns

The *memento* pattern externalizes the state of an object when you can't—or don't want to—burden the originator with implementing the storing and restoration of a particular state. Many applications record their current state so that the application can be restored to that state at a later time. Visual Basic, for example, remembers the last module that was open in the IDE and reopens it upon startup. Applications commonly implement this type of functionality by recording a snapshot of their current state in the registry or in some other external file upon the closing of the application. When the application is restarted, the application reads the state and restores itself to the recorded state. The memento pattern is used in those cases when an object or groups of objects need to store their state for later restoration or comparison.

Understanding Memento's Design

The memento pattern uses three types of objects to provide state management services for objects at run time in an object-based environment. The three objects that collaborate include:

Originator   The object whose state is being recorded.

Memento   The object in which the state is stored.

Caretaker   The object that triggers the recording of the state in the memento. The caretaker stores the memento until it is needed and also triggers the restoration of the memento.

Here is a step-by-step description of how the memento pattern works:

1. Based on how the developer has coded the caretaker object, the caretaker determines that originator may have to be restored to its current state at a later time. For instance, in a system that allows the user to change the columns in a grid, you may decide to provide *undo* functionality. In such a situation, the caretaker (which may be a *modify grid columns* button) would trigger the saving of the memento. The caretaker triggers the originator before a certain action occurs, changing the state of originator and thereby allowing the user to undo the action. Caretaker may also trigger originator when it predicts that there is a high probability that originator will fail and will have to be restored. In this situation, you may have decided that posting to a general ledger may be a high-risk action, which the user may want to undo. Again, a caretaker may trigger the creation of a memento that stores the ledger's original state.

2. After caretaker determines that originator may need to be restored later, it requests a Memento from Originator.

3. Originator instantiates and sets the properties of memento, and passes memento back to caretaker.

4. If and when originator has to be restored, caretaker passes memento back to originator.

5. Originator reads the properties of memento and restores itself to the recorded state.

Figure 20.1 depicts these steps in a sequence diagram.

FIGURE 20.1
A sequence diagram of the memento pattern

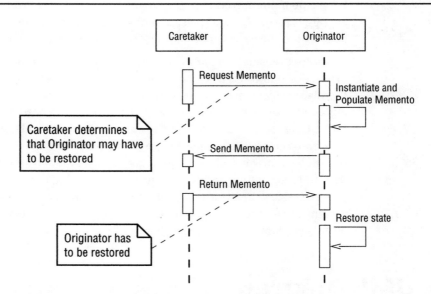

Why Separate the Saving and Storing of the Memento?

The memento pattern can help the Visual Basic designer eliminate certain pitfalls that sometimes accompany the originator object. Although you can easily implement the memento-type functionality by having the originator object record, manage, and restore its own state, this self-restoration process has drawbacks. For example:

- Originator might not record its state because it doesn't have enough awareness of its environment to determine that the state may need to restore itself.

- Originator may become bloated with peripheral memento functionality. As a result, the object contains many other objects and methods that are there only to handle state management. These extra objects and methods can confuse a developer who sees more capabilities in the object than are necessary.

To mitigate these dangers, the memento pattern delegates the responsibility of managing the recording and restoring of state to a dedicated caretaker object. This keeps the memento code in originator to a minimum. And since caretaker's job is to trigger recording and restoring of state, it can be designed to hook into the environment to the extent that it knows when to trigger a record or restore.

Another reason to separate the saving and storing of the memento is because the originator will often have protected data that needs to be stored in the memento. For instance, a Customer object may have a protected ID property (so that external objects cannot change the customer ID). However, we need that ID in our memento so that we can restore the state of the customer object at a later time! By having the originator create the memento, we have no issues with private data because the originator is always allowed to access its own data. The memento is then passed to the caretaker, which handles storing and accessing the memento as a whole whenever necessary. Restoring the private data is just as easy, since the caretaker returns the memento, as a whole, to the originator. The originator then restores all of its own data.

A UML Diagram of a Memento Pattern

Figure 20.2 illustrates how the private property Value1 of originator is externalized in a memento object but is only visible to originator and not to caretaker, even though caretaker actually manages memento. Here is how it works. Memento stores data as properties defined in an abstract interface called IMementoData. Memento implements this interface using the `Implements` keyword. Both originator and caretaker share the same instance of memento. However, caretaker declares the variable that contains the instance of memento as Memento, while originator declares it as IMementoData. This allows only originator to read and write to the IMemento properties implemented in memento.

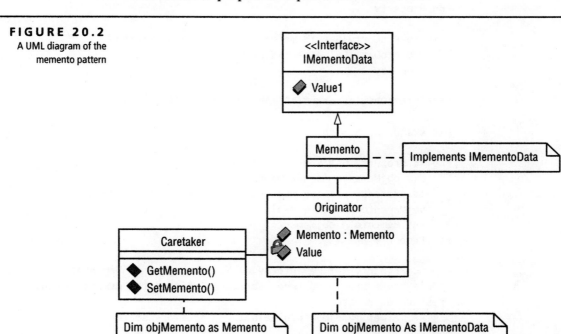

FIGURE 20.2
A UML diagram of the
memento pattern

Here is some sample code illustrating this process:

```
'*******IMementoData*****************************
Public Property Get Value1() As String

End Property

Public Property Let Value1(ByVal Value As String)

End Property

'*******Memento********************************
Implements IMementoData
Dim sValue1 As String
```

```
Private Property Let IMementoData_Value1(ByVal Value As String)
    sValue1 = Value
End Property

Private Property Get IMementoData_Value1() As String
    IMementoData_Value1 = sValue1
End Property

'*********Originator*******************************

Dim sValue As String

Public Property Get Memento() As Memento
    Dim objMemento As New Memento
'*This procedure is run when caretaker requests a memento
    objMemento.Value1 = sValue      'record state
    Set Memento = objMemento
End Property

Public Property Set Memento(ByVal MementoObject As Memento)
'*This procedure is run when caretaker returns the memento in order to
'restore originator
    Me.Value1 = objMemento.Value1      'restore state
End Property

Private Property Get Value1() As String
    Value1 = sValue
End Property

Private Property Let Value1(ByVal Value As String)
    sValue = Value
End Property

'*********Caretaker********************************
Dim objMemento As Memento
Dim objOriginator As Originator

Public Sub GetMemento()
'*This procedure is run when caretaker determines that originator's
'state must be recorded
    Set objMemento = objOriginator.Memento
End Sub
```

```
Public Sub SetMemento()
'*This procedure is run when caretaker determines that originator has
'to be restored*
    Set objOriginator.Memento = objMemento
End Sub


Public Property Set Originator(ByVal OriginatorObject As Originator)
'*This procedure is set by a client to point caretaker at an originator
    Set objOriginator = OriginatorObject
End Property
```

A Sample Use of a Memento Pattern

For our sample program, let's say we are developing a component that displays a form with a grid on it. The user is able to resize the columns of the grid, but when the form is reopened we want to restore it to its last settings. The component is part of a larger application and will be instantiated by another component.

There are two drawbacks we need to work around, however. We don't want to simply expose the grid to the client because we want to protect some of the client's properties. In addition, our component does not have permission to write to an external file or the Registry. To work around these issues, we can use the memento pattern.

Our component will externalize the column width state in a memento object. The client of our component will assume the caretaker responsibilities that are requesting, storing, and restoring the memento. Here is the code for our component:

```
'*********************Memento***************************
Dim nColwidth(5) As Integer

Public Property Get Colwidth(Index As Integer) As Integer
    Colwidth = nColwidth(Index)
End Property

Public Property Let Colwidth(Index As Integer, Value As Integer)
    nColwidth(Index) = Value
End Property
```

```
'********************GridDisplay***********************
Dim frmDisplay As New frmGrid
Dim nColwidth(5) As Integer

Public Property Get Memento() As Memento
Dim objMemento As New Memento
Dim i As Integer
With frmGrid.gDisplay
    For i = 0 To 5       'record state in memento
        objMemento.Colwidth(i) = .Colwidth(i)
    Next i
End With
Set Memento = objMemento
End Property

Public Property Set Memento(ByVal MementoObject As Memento)
Dim i As Integer
With frmGrid.gDisplay
    For i = 0 To 5       'restore state from memento
        .Colwidth(i) = objMemento.Colwidth(i)
    Next i
End With
End Property

Private Sub Class_Initialize()
frmDisplay.Show
End Sub
```

Related Patterns

Memento is commonly used with the command pattern to provide undo function-ality. The command object plays the role of caretaker by getting a memento before a certain procedure of the originator is run. If and when the undo function is needed, command—in the role of caretaker—supplies the memento to the originator.

Memento can also be used by iterator to store what point of the iteration it is at, so it can resume iterating at a later time. In other words, if we are scanning through a directory, importing files, and the user pauses the import, our directory iterator knows which file we're up to, and uses a memento to record that in a file so that it can continue at a later time.

NOTE For more on related patterns, see Chapter 14, "The Command Pattern," and Chapter 16, "The Iterator Pattern."

Conclusion

Memento is best suited for externalizing the state of an object when you can't or don't want to burden the originator with implementing the storing and restoration of state. In cases where you have to externalize protected data, the design of memento allows you to hide that data from the objects that handle it. Only originator has to access the actual data that is being externalized. The caretaker that manages the data only has to request it, store it, and return it.

chapter 21

The State Pattern

- Types of state patterns

- An example of a state pattern

- A UML diagram of a state pattern

- A sample use of a state pattern

- Other uses of a state

- Related patterns

The *state* pattern allows an object's implementation to change depending on the internal state of the object. It provides a way to alter the behavior of an object whenever the state of the object changes. To achieve this, the object delegates its behavior to encapsulated state-specific objects. The state pattern can be used in any application where an object's behavior depends on the state of the object. One example of this is a drawing application, where the behavior of the application is dependent on the drawing state that the user has selected.

Types of State Patterns

The state pattern is implemented with two different types of objects, *context objects* and *individual state objects*. The context object provides an interface for the client to access the methods of the current state object and maintains a reference to the current state object. In contrast, the state objects implement the specific functionality.

Context Objects

The criteria for transitioning between different states can be implemented in either the context object or the state object. The context object provides one central place to implement the criteria for state transitions. It is useful to implement the logic in the context object if the criteria were fixed. In this model, the context object will determine which state object is the current state of the application. The state object can be changed in response to any event, including an action by the user (clicking a button), a new token in a parser, or a different state in a protocol.

A drawing application is a good example of an application with the context object controlling the transitions between states. When a user changes the drawing tool in the application, the context object can change the current state object. If the user changes from drawing rectangles to drawing circles, the context object will receive a message notifying it of a change. The context object then changes the state object from the rectangle state object to the circle state object. The current state object is maintained as a reference in the context object. The context object is the only class to have knowledge of the different drawing state objects and it knows the criteria to transition between the different states.

Individual State Objects

The second type of state pattern decentralizes the criteria to transition between state objects. It moves this logic into the individual state objects. Each state object knows which state will occur after it. Each state object can call a method, like Set-CurrentState, on the context object to change the current state. The one disadvantage to this model is that each state object must have knowledge of at least one other state object. In the centralized view, the state objects have no knowledge that other state objects exist.

An Example of a State Pattern

An RTF parser can be implemented as a decentralized state pattern. In this example, the individual state objects would contain the criteria to transition to the next state. As the parser is moving through the RTF code, the state object would recognize a change from one state to another. It can then notify the context object that a change in state has occurred by setting the current state object to another state subclass.

In RTF, there are several different states that a parser can be in when it is moving through the code. The parser can handle plain text and can control tokens like bold, underline, and fonts; it can parse arguments for a control token like the font size; or it can handle special characters like alpha or beta. If the parser was in the plain text state, that is to say it was processing text that will appear in the final document, and the parser reaches a backslash, then the state object would recognize this as a transition to a different state. The backslash is the character used to denote the beginning of a control word. The state object can call the SetCurrentState method on the context object and pass a reference to a control state object.

In this example, the context object provides an interface for the client to call methods implemented in the state objects and it stores a reference to the current state. It contains no code to determine the transitions between states. All of this transitional logic is contained in the individual state objects.

A UML Diagram of a State Pattern

Figure 21.1 depicts a standard implementation of the state pattern. A context object aggregates the functionality defined within the individual state objects. For each state within the context object, there exists one concrete state object. The context delegates state-specific behavior to the state objects. The state objects provide an atomic view of the behavior of each state.

FIGURE 21.1
An object model of a state
pattern

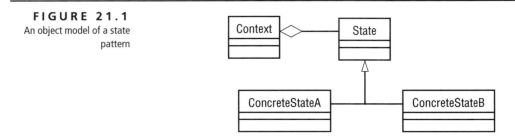

The context object maintains the current state. This means that a reference to the current state object is maintained within the context object. Whenever a request is made of the context object it forwards that request to the current state object. It is then up to the state object to fulfill the request.

In Figure 21.2, a state pattern is depicted within a drawing application. Here, the drawing context receives events from the user that allows it to change its internal state. Once the state is changed and the user proceeds to draw shapes on the form, these messages are forwarded to the appropriate state object. Each state object encapsulates the methods for drawing a particular shape on the form.

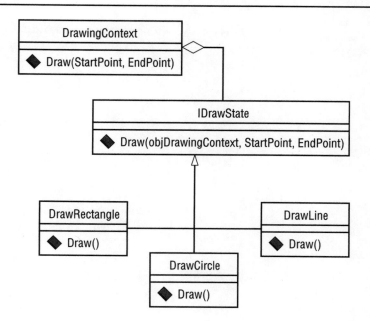

FIGURE 21.2
A state pattern imple-
mented within a drawing
application

A Sample Use of a State Pattern

Let's take a look at the drawing application that we have designed above. Figure 21.3 shows the user interface of the drawing application. The user interface consists of a toolbar and a drawing surface. The toolbar stores the current state of the application. The application can either be in a default, rectangle, line, square, or circle drawing state.

FIGURE 21.3
A drawing application
using the state pattern

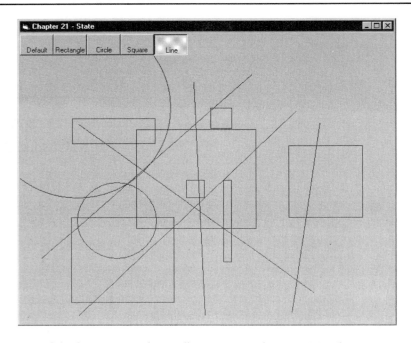

Pressing one of the buttons on the toolbar triggers the transition between states. This changes the state within the DrawingContext. The following code switches the current state object of the DrawingContext.

```
' DrawingContext class
Private objState As IDrawState
Private intCurrentState As CurrentState

Public Enum CurrentState
    drwDefault
    drwRectangle
    drwCircle
    drwSquare
    drwLine
End Enum
```

```
Public Property Let State(value As CurrentState)
    intCurrentState = value

    Select Case intCurrentState
        Case drwDefault
            Set objState = New DrawDefault
        Case drwRectangle
            Set objState = New DrawRectangle
        Case drwCircle
            Set objState = New DrawCircle
        Case drwSquare
            Set objState = New DrawSquare
        Case drwLine
            Set objState = New DrawLine
    End Select
End Property
```

Once the current state is set, shapes can be drawn on the canvas. You accomplish this by delegating the Draw messages from the DrawingContext to the appropriate state object.

```
' DrawingContext class
Public Sub Draw(pntStart As point, pntEnd As point)
    objState.Draw Me, pntStart, pntEnd
End Sub
```

Here the draw method of the DrawingContext just calls the Draw method of the state object. One thing to note is that the DrawingContext passes a reference from itself to the state object. This allows the state objects to access the properties of the drawing context. This would also be the way to implement a more decentralized version of the state pattern; one in which each state object controls the transitions between states.

The state objects encapsulate how to draw the different shapes. Here is the code from the DrawRectangle class.

```
Implements IDrawState

Private Sub IDrawState_Draw(objDraw As DrawingContext, _
        StartPoint As point, EndPoint As point)
    objDraw.CurrentForm.Line (StartPoint.x, StartPoint.y) _
        -(EndPoint.x, EndPoint.y), , B
End Sub
```

As you can see, the code here is rather simple. This simplicity is achieved because the code is partitioned in a different object for each state. This allows new states to be added without interfering with the code of other states.

Other Uses of a State

The state pattern is ideal for handling both classes with a few states and classes with a large number of states. By partitioning the code for each state in a separate object, the state pattern can scale well when a large number of states are needed. This is the state pattern's purpose, to partition the code for states.

An application-specific use for the state pattern could be in tracking the state of an asynchronous operation, like opening an ADO recordset asynchronously. The context object could store the current state of the operation and delegate any method calls to state-specific classes.

Related Patterns

You can use the singleton pattern to implement a state object. The singleton pattern allows multiple context objects to share a single state object. The singleton pattern enforces that only one state object exists.

Another way to share state objects is by using the flyweight pattern. The flyweight pattern externalizes the context of a state object, which allows the state object to be reused in many contexts. Whenever methods are called on the state object, the current state context is passed into the method, so the state object does not have to store these properties. This allows the state object to be reused in many contexts without sharing the settings between contexts.

NOTE For more on related patterns, see Chapter 9, "The Flyweight Pattern," and Chapter 24, "The Singleton Pattern."

Conclusion

The state pattern is ideal for implementing classes whose behavior is dependent on state. It is ideal for separating the complexity that often exists with code that transitions between many states. It provides a mechanism to scale state machines since the code for each state is isolated within its own object.

chapter 22

The Strategy Pattern

- Means of implementing strategy patterns

- A UML diagram of a strategy pattern

- A sample use of a strategy pattern

- Related patterns

The *strategy* pattern abstracts a family of algorithms into individual objects that share a common interface so that the objects can be used interchangeably. A family of algorithms is a group of calculations that aim to solve the same problem in different ways. For example, consider an application that computes tax liabilities based on a tax bracket. Depending on the given tax bracket, different calculations are used. The calculations as a group form a family of algorithms that aim to compute tax liability. You would typically implement this functionality in an application by using a parameterized procedure that branches out to the appropriate calculation based on the value of the parameters.

Strategy offers an alternative, object-oriented solution. A common interface known as strategy is defined for the tax calculation. Each one of the calculations is encapsulated into an individual object that implements strategy. These objects are known as *concrete strategy objects*. The client is bound to the strategy interface and based on the given criterion is set to use one of the concrete strategy objects. By using object orientation and design patterns, you gain the following benefits:

- You can use simpler modules instead of dense parameterized procedures. Weigh this benefit against the drawback—an increase in the number of objects in the system.

- You can easily include or exclude specific strategies in a project.

- You can add new strategies with a minimal modification to the client and no modification to the server objects.

An interesting way to think about the Strategy pattern is that it is the implementation half of the bridge pattern. Remember that the bridge pattern attempts to decouple an interface from an implementation by having the client bound to the interface use one of a family of implementation objects. Strategy follows this theme and turns each member of the family of algorithms into an individual implementation object.

Means of Implementing Strategy Patterns

There is one type of strategy with two means of implementation. Some strategy objects may require more or different information than others. The varying implementations focus on how to provide the strategy objects with the information they require. You can accomplish this transfer of data in two ways:

- Pass any data needed for any of the calculations to all the strategy objects. The obvious drawback of this approach is that the client will have to pass all parameters, even if the specific strategy object doesn't use them. With Visual Basic you can make some parameters Optional. However, then the client has to be smart enough to know which parameters its current strategy object requires.

- Pass the object that contains all the necessary information to the strategy object, and have the strategy object look up the information it needs. The drawback of this approach is that the object being passed in has to surface all the information in its public interface. And the strategy objects have to know the object's interface in order to read its properties.

If you have a well defined interface that will not change with the passage of time, the first option will often make the most sense since it is easier to understand (VB's intellisense will show you all of the parameters). However, if the interface requires the addition of more information over time, passing an object allows you to standardize the parameter passing while enhancing the passed object, so the latter option will often be preferred.

A UML Diagram of a Strategy Pattern

As you can see from Figure 22.1, a strategy pattern defines an abstract interface for a group of calculations. Each one of the calculations is abstracted into an individual object which conforms to the abstract interface. The client object is bound to the abstract interface and can be set to use any one of the concrete strategy objects.

NOTE   For an explanation on how to define and implement abstract interfaces using Visual Basic's `Implements` keyword, see Chapter 3, "Visual Basic and Design Patterns."

FIGURE 22.1
A UML diagram of a
strategy pattern

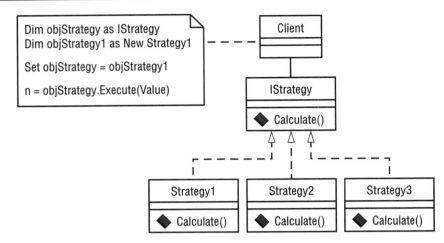

A Sample Use of a Strategy Pattern

For our sample, we'll create a simple application that allows the user to switch between drawing zigzag lines and dashed lines. The application consists of a form, an abstract interface called ILine, and concrete strategy classes called LineZag and LineDash. ILine has one public function called CalculatePoints. This public function takes two horizontal points as parameters and returns a two-dimensional array intended to contain the x and y points needed to draw a line. LineDash and LineZag encapsulate the algorithms that calculate the x/y points for zigzag and dashed lines respectively. The form allows the user to choose between the two types of lines, and drag the mouse forward to create a line of the desired type. When the user chooses a type of line, a variable declared as ILine is pointed to reference an instance of the appropriate concrete strategy class, either LineZag or LineDash. Here's the code:

```
'*******************
'ILine- abstract interface
Public Function CalculatePoints(X1 As Long, X2 As Long) As Long()

End Function
'*******************
```

```
'LineZig
Implements ILine

Private Function ILine_CalculatePoints(X1 As Long, X2 As Long) As
Long()
  Dim Y As Integer
  Dim X As Long
  Dim nPeak As Integer
  Dim nDirection As Integer
  Dim lngPoints() As Long
  ReDim lngPoints(X1 - 1 To X2 - 1, 1)

  nDirection = 1
  nPeak = 50
  Y = 0
  For X = X1 To X2
      If Y > nPeak Then
          nDirection = -1
      ElseIf Y < -nPeak Then
          nDirection = 1
      End If
      Y = Y + nDirection
      lngPoints(X - 1, 0) = X
      lngPoints(X - 1, 1) = Y
  Next X
  ILine_CalculatePoints = lngPoints
End Function
'*************************
'LineDash
Implements ILine

Private Function ILine_CalculatePoints(X1 As Long, X2 As Long) As _
Long()
  Dim X As Long
  Dim nLength As Integer
  Dim nSpace As Integer
  Dim lngPoints() As Long
  Dim i As Integer
  Dim n As Integer
  ReDim lngPoints(X2- X1 - 1, 1)
```

```
nLength = 40
nSpace = 20
X = X1
n = 0
For i = 1 To (X2 - X1)
    If n > nLength Then
        n = 0
        X = X + nSpace
    Else
        X = X + 1
    End If
    If X > X2 Then Exit For
    lngPoints(i - 1, 0) = X
    lngPoints(i - 1, 1) = 1
    n = n + 1
Next i
ILine_CalculatePoints = lngPoints
End Function
    '*****************************************
'client form
Dim beginX As Long
Dim endX As Long
Dim objLine As ILine
Dim objLineDash As New LineDash
Dim objLineZig As New LineZig

Private Sub Form_Load()
optLineType(0).Value = True
End Sub

Private Sub Form_MouseDown(Button As Integer, Shift As Integer, X As
Single, Y As Single)
  beginX = X
End Sub

Private Sub Form_MouseUp(Button As Integer, Shift As Integer, X As
Single, Y As Single)
  Dim vPoints As Variant
  Dim i As Long
```

```
If X > beginX Then
    vPoints = objLine.CalculatePoints(CLng(beginX), CLng(X))
    CurrentY = Y
    For i = LBound(vPoints) To UBound(vPoints)
        CurrentX = vPoints(i, 0) - 1

Line -(vPoints(i, 0), (vPoints(i, 1)) + Y)
    Next i
End If
End Sub

Private Sub optLineType_Click(Index As Integer)
Select Case True
Case optLineType(0)
    Set objLine = objLineDash
Case optLineType(1)
    Set objLine = objLineZig
End Select
End Sub
```

Related Patterns

Strategy is essentially the second half of a bridge pattern. The bridge allows the application to bind the client to one interface and dynamically alter the implementation object. Strategy complements bridge by defining a group of objects. This group encapsulates varying algorithms that aim to solve a common problem.

If the use of strategy adds too many objects to the system, then you can use a flyweight to manage them. This will allow you to use many objects without having to worry about the extra memory and system resources that would be used.

NOTE For more on related patterns, see Chapter 4, "The Bridge Pattern," and Chapter 9, "The Flyweight Pattern."

Conclusion

The strategy pattern is best suited for when an application chooses from a family of algorithms to solve a particular problem. You should especially consider choosing a strategy pattern when a parameterized procedure—based on the value of a parameter—chooses the appropriate algorithm to apply. Strategy calls for the separate algorithms to be encapsulated in individual objects that conform to a common interface. The client is bound to the strategy interface and can be dynamically pointed to use any one of the individual strategy objects. Note that in addition to implementing calculations as strategies, processes can be thought of as strategies as well, allowing us to bind our clients to different processes as needed.

Creational Patterns

chapter 23

The Factory Pattern

- Methods of implementing a factory pattern

- A UML diagram of a factory pattern

- A sample use of a factory pattern

- Other uses of a factory

- Related patterns

The *factory* pattern provides a mechanism to separate a client from the process of creating a set of related objects or products. It provides an interface to delegate the creation of objects without specifying the concrete class. The factory encapsulates the rules for instantiating objects and buffers the client from the knowledge of the concrete class that is being instantiated.

By eliminating the client's knowledge of the concrete classes being instantiated, the factory pattern allows the application to instantiate different objects at run time, as long as the concrete classes all conform to the same interface. As a result, depending on the variable or parameter, the application can change its look by instantiating different visual controls on the user interface. Another, non-visual example, is that the factory pattern can instantiate different objects to perform a calculation, which would allow the application to vary the calculation in certain situations.

Methods of Implementing a Factory Pattern

The factory pattern can be implemented in two ways, either by defining different methods for instantiating each product or by creating a parameterized method for instantiating all of the products. In the first case, an interface is often designed where each product is created by one method. The following code implements this type of interface for a charting application. The client application would explicitly request a different type of chart using the different functions, MakeBarChart, MakePieChart, MakeLineChart:

```
' Class AbstractFactory
Public Function MakeBarChart() As BarChart
End Function

Public Function MakePieChart() As PieChart
End Function

Public Function MakeLineChart() As LineChart
End Function
```

The main problem with defining the abstract factory in this manner is that whenever a new product is added to the application, the interface and all of the subclasses must be modified. This will often cause problems with compatibility between versions of the factory class.

The second method of implementing the factory pattern is to provide one method for creating the products; then pass a parameter to this method to distinguish which product is to be instantiated. Parameterizing the factory allows new products to be added to the group without changing the interface of the factory. Instead of having a different method for each concrete class, a parameterized method is created to return a different concrete class. The client calls one method and passes in a parameter to determine which concrete class will be instantiated.

The following example changes the charting application shown above into a parameterized factory method. Instead of having three methods that return a different concrete class, there is one method, called MakeChart, that returns a different concrete class, which is based on the Chart interface.

```
' Class ConcreteFactory
Enum products
    prdPieChart
    prdBarChart
    prdLineChart
End Enum

Public Function MakeChart(ChartType As products) As Chart
    Select Case ChartType
        Case prdPieChart
            Set MakeChart = New PieChart
        Case prdBarChart
            Set MakeChart = New BarChart
        Case prdLineChart
            Set MakeChart = New LineChart
    End Select
End Function
```

The products of the MakeChart method (PieChart, BarChart, and LineChart) inherit the interface of the Chart class. This is one of the limitations of the parameterized factory. All products must implement the same abstract base class. If class-specific variations exist in the products, then it is up to the client to cast the product into the correct class. However, this defeats one of the purposes of creating the factory, namely to separate the client from the concrete classes being instantiated.

A UML Diagram of a Factory Pattern

Figure 23.1 shows an abstract implementation of the factory pattern. It is implemented by using a different method for each concrete class.

FIGURE 23.1
A UML diagram of the
factory pattern

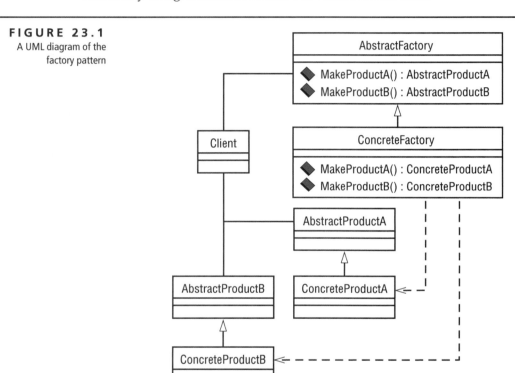

In this model, the MakeProductA method of ConcreteFactory would instantiate and return a reference to a ConcreteProductA object; the MakeProductB method would instantiate and return a reference to a ConcreteProductB object.

Figure 23.1 shows the inflexibility inherent in this method of implementing the factory pattern. For each new product added to the product family, a new method must be created in the abstract factory, as well as all of the subclasses. By adding this new method, the signature of the class's interface has changed. If you implement these classes as an ActiveX DLL, then the DLL will lose binary compatibility with previous versions and will necessitate recompiling the client application.

The more flexible method of implementing the factory pattern as a parameter-ized method is depicted in Figure 23.2. The parameterized factory allows for a clean interface, but can limit the functionality present in each of the products since they all must conform to the same interface.

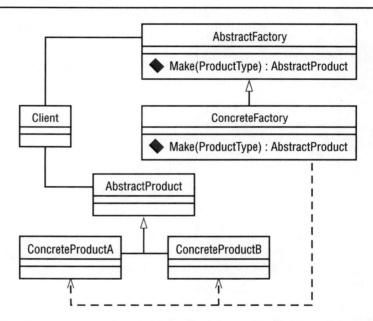

The downside to implementing the factory pattern as a parameterized method is that the interface for the product classes (ConcreteProductA, ConcreteProductB) become inflexible. Adding new functionality to the interface of one product means modifying the interface and code of all of the related products. In order to determine which implementation is appropriate for your application, you will need to determine what is more likely to change, the number of products in the family of related products, or the interfaces of the individual products. If you find that you will likely add new product classes to your application, then the parame-terized method is a better solution. If you find that the interfaces for the product classes varies and/or will vary in the future, then the first implementation is more appropriate, that of creating a separate method for each product.

In addition to decoupling the client from the concrete classes that the factory creates, the factory pattern allows hook methods to be added to the process of cre-ating an object. Figure 23.3 depicts a hook method after instantiating the product object.

FIGURE 23.3
The hook method imple-
mented in a factory pattern

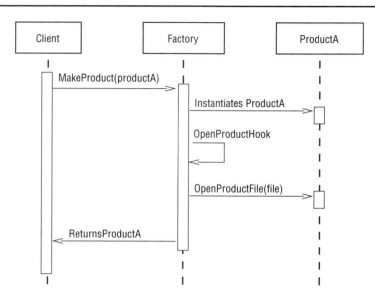

By implementing the hook method within the factory, the factory can provide the client with an extended version of the product. In the example of the charts, the hook method could open a file dialog box to allow the user to select a file containing the data for a chart. The hook would then populate the chart with this data before the chart is returned to the client. The client application would then just need to display the chart, and not have any knowledge of how the chart is stored.

NOTE   For more on the hook method, see Chapter 19, "The Hook Pattern."

A Sample Use of a Factory Pattern

Graphical applications are useful for demonstrating the factory pattern. In the following section the factory pattern is implemented within a charting application. The factory pattern is a powerful abstraction to use within a charting application because it allows the user interface to vary, but the code to display the chart can remain the same. The factory pattern allows a client application to vary the look of data just by passing a different parameter into a method. The following example will implement the basic functionality of a charting tool using the factory method to create the different charts as products of the factory.

Figure 23.4 shows the user interface for the sample. The application is composed of five class modules and a form. The form is the client to the factory. It asks the factory to create a chart and then asks the chart to display itself. The form has no knowledge of how the chart is displayed, nor does it have knowledge of which class is displaying the chart.

FIGURE 23.4
A charting tool using the factory pattern

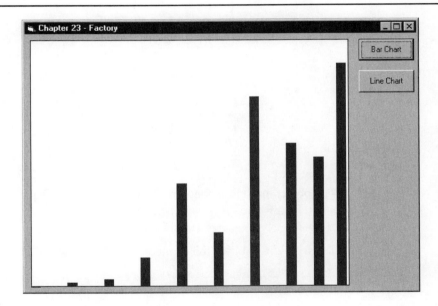

FIGURE 23.5
An object model of a
charting tool

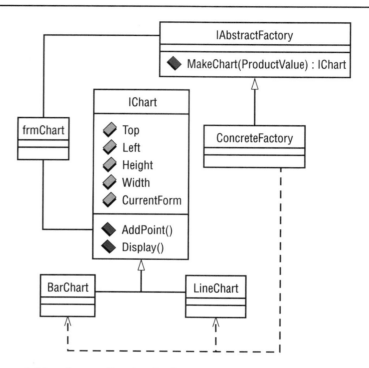

The object model for the application is shown in Figure 23.5. The two abstract classes, IChart and IAbstractFactory, define the interfaces for the chart products and the ConcreteFactory class.

The following shows the implementation of the code of the ConcreteFactory.

```
Implements IAbstractFactory

Private Function IAbstractFactory_MakeChart(ChartType _
    As products) As IChart
    Select Case ChartType
        Case prdBarChart
            Set IAbstractFactory_MakeChart = New BarChart
        Case prdLineChart
            Set IAbstractFactory_MakeChart = New LineChart
    End Select
End Function
```

All the code does is return a new instance of chart based on the parameter that was passed to the MakeChart function. The client code that calls this function is shown below.

```
Private objFactory As Factory.IAbstractFactory
Private objChart As iChart

Private Sub cmdBarChart_Click()
    Me.Cls
    Set objFactory = New Factory.ConcreteFactory
    Set objChart = objFactory.MakeChart(prdBarChart)
    DisplayChart
End Sub

Private Sub cmdLineChart_Click()
    Me.Cls
    Set objFactory = New Factory.ConcreteFactory
    Set objChart = objFactory.MakeChart(prdLineChart)
    DisplayChart
End Sub
```

The code shows that the objChart is dimensioned as IChart. This means the client does not know which concrete class is being returned from the MakeChart function. Since all of the product classes (BarChart and LineChart) implement the same interface, the client code does not need to know what concrete class is being returned.

Other Uses of a Factory

The factory pattern is good for providing a mechanism for instantiating a set of related objects. Often times the factory pattern is used to alter the user interface of an application, as in the sample application demonstrated above. The factory pattern is not limited to user interfaces, however. You can also use it to change business objects. Take a tax application, for example. Depending on where you live, there are different rules for calculating the taxes. A factory pattern could be used to return a tax class that is dependent on your location.

Related Patterns

The factory method pattern is often used with the factory pattern. In our examples, the factory method was used to determine which concrete class to instantiate and return to the client.

The singleton pattern is also associated with the factory pattern. The factory pattern is often implemented as a singleton because only one instance of the factory object is needed within an application. The purpose of the singleton pattern is to ensure that only one instance of an object exists at any time. By implementing the factory object as a singleton, only one instance of the factory object would exist at any time.

NOTE   Learn more about a related pattern in Chapter 24, "The Singleton Pattern."

Conclusion

The factory pattern is best suited for implementations where a set of related objects are used in an application. The factory pattern is ideal at separating the client application from the details of the related products. In order to provide the most flexibility in the factory pattern, these related objects should all implement the same interface and not provide any extra class-specific interfaces.

chapter 24

The Singleton Pattern

- Means of implementing singleton patterns

- A UML diagram of a singleton pattern

- A sample use of a singleton pattern

- Other uses of a singleton

- Related patterns

The *singleton* pattern ensures that only one instance of a class exists at any time. It forces client applications to work with only one instance of a class and will not allow them to instantiate more then one instance. It provides a single, global point of access for clients to work with a resource. The singleton pattern is a powerful pattern to share a resource among multiple clients, but the truth is that there is no elegant and safe implementation in VB. Since VB hides all of the details of instantiating objects and keeping count of the object references, VB has no way to implement the singleton pattern as it is described by the Gang of Four.

The issue that arises when trying to implement the singleton pattern in VB is that VB hides the process of instantiating objects. VB only fires the Class_Initialize event after the class has been instantiated. In addition, COM does not allow external programs to gain access to the reference count of an object. And even if it did, the COM specification only guarantees the reference count is correct when it is zero. Therefore, the COM reference count cannot be used to implement the singleton pattern. So a VB application has no idea how many references there are to an object and it only knows after the fact that the object has been created.

Means of Implementing Singleton Patterns

Although there are severe limitations to using the singleton pattern with Visual Basic, you can use VB to approximate the functionality inherent in the singleton pattern. This chapter will present three different types of implementations for the singleton pattern. The three implementations will be a singleton built into a standard EXE, a singleton built into an ActiveX DLL, and a singleton built into an ActiveX EXE. Each implementation offers varying degrees of flexibility.

Singleton in a Standard EXE

A singleton can be a very useful pattern inside a Standard EXE. In its simplest form, you can use it as a place to store variables throughout an application. The implementation is based on mimicking the AddRef method of the IUnknown interface of COM inside the class module. When the singleton class is instantiated, the reference count is incremented by one and checked to ensure that only one instance exists. Within the Class_Initialize method of the singleton object is the following code:

```
Private Sub Class_Initialize()
    basSingleton.AddRef
    basSingleton.CheckInstance Me
End Sub
```

This code calls two methods stored in a global module, AddRef and Check-Instance. The code for these methods are shown below:

```
' basSingleton - global module
Public Const E_REF_COUNT_EXCEEDED = vbObjectError + 512 + 1
Public Const EXCEED_ERROR_MESSAGE = _
          "There can only be one instance of the clsSingleton class."

Private m_iSingletonCount As Integer
Private m_oSingleton As clsSingleton

Public Sub AddRef()
    If m_iSingletonCount = 1 Then
        Err.Raise E_REF_COUNT_EXCEEDED, _
                   "Singleton.basSingleton.AddRef", _
                   EXCEED_ERROR_MESSAGE
    End If

    m_iSingletonCount = m_iSingletonCount + 1
End Sub

Public Sub CheckInstance(oSingleton As clsSingleton)
    If m_oSingleton Is Nothing Then
        Set m_oSingleton = oSingleton
    End If
End Sub
```

The AddRef method ensures that only one instance of the class exists at any one time by storing the reference count in the variable m_iSingletonCount. The Check-Instance method is used to protect against the client from instantiating the class directly with:

```
Dim oSingleton as clsSingleton
Set oSingleton = New clsSingleton
```

Whenever this code is called, the application will ensure that no other instance exists. If no instance exists, the CheckInstance method stores a reference to the singleton in the global module. If a second client tries to instantiate the singleton class using the New keyword, they will get an error, so the application must provide another interface for accessing the singleton. You can do this by adding a GetSingleton method to the basSingleton global module as follows:

```
Public Function GetSingleton() As clsSingleton
    If m_oSingleton Is Nothing Then
        Set m_oSingleton = New clsSingleton
    End If

    Set GetSingleton = m_oSingleton
End Function
```

The GetSingleton method provides another point of access for clients to retrieve a reference to the singleton object. This would be the preferred method of access to the singleton pattern. The point of access through the New keyword is to provide a level of safety to the application.

Missing from this discussion thus far is the process of releasing the reference. This is a difficult topic because no method exists to accurately track the number of references to a given object. If every client were to retrieve a reference to the singleton object through these two methods—GetSingleton and CheckInstance— then the application can keep the count. However, client applications don't necessarily need to use these two methods. They can pass around a reference through a third method, with code like the following:

```
Dim oSingleton As clsSingleton
Dim oSecond As clsSingleton

Set oSingleton = New clsSingleton
Set oSecond = oSingleton
```

In this example, the global module would only think that one reference exists. In reality, though, there would be two. Since VB does not raise any event when another reference to an existing object is made, there is no way to accurately count how many references to the object exist. For this reason, you cannot automatically destroy a singleton object.

Singleton in an ActiveX DLL

By moving the singleton object into an ActiveX DLL, the interface to the singleton is simplified. The simplification is achieved through the use of the instancing property of the class, which eliminates the need to access the singleton through the New keyword. In an ActiveX DLL, there would be two classes, one called clsSingleton and another called clsSingletonManager. The instancing property of the clsSingleton class would be set to PublicNotCreatable. The instancing property of clsSingletonManager would be set to GlobalMultiUse. You use this class to mimic the functionality that was encapsulated within the global module of the Standard EXE example above since functions of a global module cannot be exposed from a COM component.

The implementation now gets reduced to a GetInstance method in the clsSingletonManager class. The code is as follows:

```
Public Function GetSingleton() As clsSingleton
    If g_oSingleton Is Nothing Then
        Set g_oSingleton = New clsSingleton
    End If

    Set GetSingleton = g_oSingleton
End Function
```

The variable g_oSingleton is a public variable stored in a global module. It provides a global reference to the singleton instance.

Since the clsSingleton class is declared as PublicNotCreatable, you don't need to check the reference count from the Class_Initialize event. Removing the need to check if the instance was created from the client using the New keyword provides a cleaner implementation and simplifies the interface for working with the singleton object. By declaring the class as PublicNotCreateable, you make the VB compiler enforce the rule that does not allow any client application to instantiate the singleton object using the New keyword. This means that clients cannot instantiate the singleton object with code like the following:

```
Dim oSingleton As clsSingleton
Set oSingleton = New clsSingleton
```

Since there is no accurate method for tracking how many references exist to the instance of an object, it is again unnecessary to track the number of references created through the GetSingleton method. As in the Standard EXE example above, since the singleton object does not know how many clients have a reference to it, there is no way to automatically destroy the singleton object.

Singleton in an ActiveX EXE

Moving the singleton to an ActiveX EXE allows multiple applications to share one instance of a class. Since the ActiveX Exe runs in its own memory space, the singleton class can be shared between the multiple applications. This sharing allows you to create a global resource for multiple clients. A good use for the singleton pattern in an ActiveX EXE would be to provide connection pooling toa suite of applications. The implementation of the singleton in the ActiveX EXE is the same as for the ActiveX DLL.

A UML Diagram of a Singleton Pattern

The object model for the singleton pattern is probably the simplest model, as shown in Figure 24.1. In its abstract form, the implementation of the singleton pattern would be as clean as that shown in Figure 24.1. There is one class that can have a cardinality of one. Multiple clients can access that one instance of the singleton.

FIGURE 24.1
An object model of a
singleton pattern

The exact implementation of the singleton pattern in VB, however, is somewhat different from this pure model. The implementation of singleton in the ActiveX DLL and ActiveX EXE would look like the model depicted in Figure 24.2. This object model shows the relationship that the clsSingletonManager plays within the application. It acts as the global access point to the one singleton object through the GetSingleton method.

FIGURE 24.2
A singleton pattern as
implemented in a VB
ActiveX DLL or ActiveX EXE

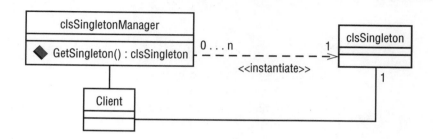

A Sample Use of a Singleton Pattern

You can use the singleton pattern to encapsulate anything currently implemented within a global module. You can use it to store a global database connection or to provide connection pooling to clients. In addition, you can use the singleton to provide a repository of variables that can be used across an application session. The following sample will implement a rudimentary database connection pooling class. The object model for this scenario is shown in Figure 24.3.

FIGURE 24.3
The singleton pattern
implemented for
connection pooling

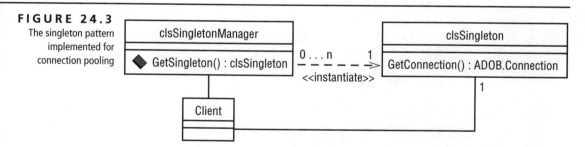

The implementation of the singleton object is the same as described in the section, "Singleton in an ActiveX DLL." The only addition is this public function GetConnection. This method iterates through a collection of connections and finds the one that is currently open and not in the process of executing a SQL statement. The code for this is as follows:

```
' clsSingleton
Private oCollection As Collection
Private Const S_CONNECTION_STRING As String = _
        "Provider=SQLOLEDB;Server=spi15c;Database=pubs;uid=sa"
```

```
Public Function GetConnection() As ADODB.Connection
    Dim oConn As ADODB.Connection

    For Each oConn In oCollection
        If oConn.State = adStateOpen Then
            Set GetConnection = oConn
            Exit Function
        End If
    Next

    Set oConn = New ADODB.Connection
    OpenConnection oConn
    oCollection.Add oConn
    Set GetConnection = oConn
End Function

Private Sub OpenConnection(oConn As ADODB.Connection)
    On Error GoTo Err_Handler

    oConn.Open S_CONNECTION_STRING
Exit Sub
Err_Handler:
    Err.Raise vbErrorObject + 512 + 1, _
            "clsSingleton.OpenConnection", _
            "Error opening connection"
End Sub

Private Sub Class_Initialize()
    Set oCollection = New Collection
End Sub
```

In this code, the connection pooling algorithm simply passes to a client a reference to a connection that is currently not being used. More code would have to be added to close the connections if those connections have not been used recently, so ghost connections to the database don't stay open forever.

Other Uses of a Singleton

There are many uses for the singleton pattern. The above sample shows a simple connection-pooling class, but any type of functionality that is currently implemented in global modules can be moved to a singleton class. The power of the global module is that variables within global modules are scoped to the application and that all clients can reference the variables or methods without instantiating a new class. The weakness of the global modules is that they cannot expose public variables or methods in an ActiveX DLL or ActiveX EXE. Global modules are also not object oriented. The singleton pattern overcomes the weaknesses of the global modules and still allows the client to gain the power of the global module.

Related Patterns

You can use the singleton pattern in a number of other patterns. Often the abstract factory and builder patterns are implemented as singleton objects. In most applications, however, it is only necessary to have one instance of the abstract factory or builder objects at any one time. Having only one instance of the builder or factory objects provides clients with a global point of access to retrieve product objects.

NOTE   Learn more about related pattern in Chapter 23, "The Factory Pattern," and Chapter 25, "The Builder Pattern."

Conclusion

The singleton pattern is a powerful pattern for moving an application towards a more object-oriented architecture. It allows developers to move away from global modules. It provides a single resource for multiple clients to access and offers the client a global point of access to the resource. The implementations described in this chapter are lacking from the fact that there is no accurate way to destroy the singleton object. The reason for this is that VB has no accurate way to track the number of references that currently exist in an object. Even with this limitation, there are many applications that can benefit from the implementation of the singleton pattern.

chapter 25

The Builder Pattern

- A UML diagram of a builder pattern

- A sample use of a builder pattern

- Sample code for a builder pattern

- Related patterns

The *builder* pattern is used for building products such as other objects. The interface of the builder object that builds the product is separated from its implementation. As a result, the same interface can be used to build different types of products. This allows you to modify the implementation of a builder without breaking existing clients, as well as to easily add implementations that will be compatible with existing clients. For example, let's say you are working with data that is exported to a text file. However, you want to turn the file into a more meaningful representation of the data, such as an ADO recordset, HTML report, or Excel spreadsheet. You can use builder to define an interface for building objects out of the text file and to create multiple implementations. The clients of your component only have to know one interface. At the same time, you can add as many implementations as you want.

Builder is typically used to build complex objects that require a multistep process. The builder pattern exposes each step of the process as a public method so that the object directing the builder (known as director) can have fine control over the building process. For example, let's say the data export contains multiple sets of data that have parent-child relationships. You want to give the director control over whether to build only the parents data sets, or both the child and parent sets, as the user prefers. The builder would expose both BuildParents and BuildChildren methods, thereby giving the director control of the building process. Moreover, the builder has a GetProduct method that allows the director to retrieve the product at any step in the process.

A UML Diagram of a Builder Pattern

Figure 25.1 depicts a UML diagram of a builder pattern. As you can see from the diagram, the director directs the builder to construct its product in a step-by-step manner. Note that the product object does not implement an abstract interface because, typically, products differ one from another and have their own intrinsic interfaces that the client has to access. Consider the data export example, where the text file is built into an HTML file and an Excel spreadsheet. There is no point in having both those outputs implement a common interface because to handle the product, the client has to know how to access the HTML and Excel object models, respectively. If, on the other hand, there is a common functionality among all products, then it may make sense to have both of them implement the same interface so that the client can treat them the same way.

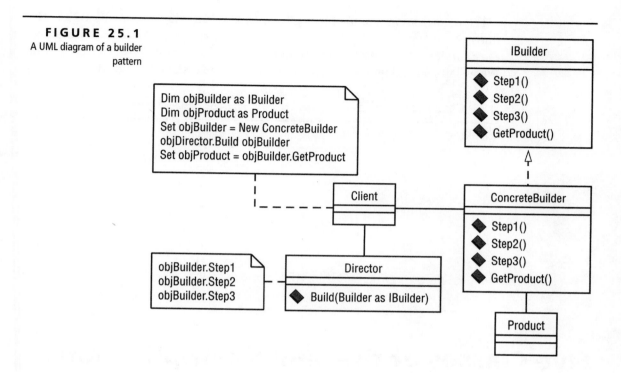

FIGURE 25.1
A UML diagram of a builder
pattern

A Sample Use of a Builder Pattern

For our sample pattern, we will use the data export scenario mentioned in the beginning of the chapter. We are working with data that is exported to a text file. The data exported consists of invoice records and their line items. Each line item has a parentid field that links to the primary key field of an invoice.

TABLE 25.1:   Table 25.1: Invoice in a tab and carriage return delimited text format

&parent			
Identification	*Customer*	*Number of Items*	*Total*
1	John Smith	3	120
2	Sam Jones	2	456
3	Mike Johnson	1	899

The invoice section of the file begins with &parent, as shown in Table 25.1. The line item section of the file begins with &child, as shown in Table 25.2. Columns are delimited by tab characters and new records are delimited by carriage returns. We will implement builders that turn the data into HTML tables and ADO recordset.

TABLE 25.2: Table 25.2: Line item record in a tab and carriage return delimited text format

&child		
Parentid	Item	Amount
1	Camera	40
1	Camera	40
1	Camera	40
2	Video Camera	200
2	CD Player	256
3	Desktop Computer	899

Five Classes of the Sample Application

Our sample application consists of five classes: Client, IBuilder, Director, HTMLBuilder, and ADOBuilder.

Client   The client initiates the building process and retrieves the product. It performs the following steps:

1. Instantiates a concrete builder

2. Configures director to use the instance of concrete builder

3. Commands director to create the product

4. Retrieves the product from the concrete builder

Figure 25.2 depicts these steps in a sequence diagram.

FIGURE 25.2
A sequence diagram depicting the steps taken to implement the sample builder pattern

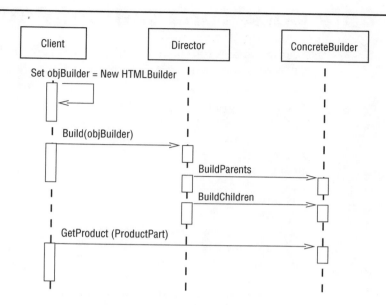

IBuilder   IBuilder is the abstract interface for building alternate representations of the text file. It has BuildParent and BuildChild methods, which build representations of the invoices and line items respectively. It also has a GetProduct method that returns either the parent, child, or both parent and child representations based on a method parameter. Note that GetProduct is typed as Variant so that it can return different types of products.

Director   The director class steps IBuilder through the building process.

HTMLBuilder   This class is a concrete class of IBuilder and produces the invoices and line items as html tables. All the invoices are in one table. Each invoice has a hyperlink to a table containing its invoices. It can build the invoice and line item tables separately.

ADOBuilder   This class is a concrete class of IBuilder and produces two recordsets one for invoices and one for line items. The recordsets are linked through their primary/foreign key relationship. It can build the invoice and line item recordsets separately.

Sample Code for a Builder Pattern

Here is the code for the sample builder. Note how the code used by the client to create both the HTML and ADO representations are nearly identical.

```
'*************Client Class*******************
Dim objDirector As New Director
Dim objBuilder As IBuilder
Dim sHTMLParent
Dim sHTMLChild
Dim sHTMLBoth
Dim rsChild
Dim rsParent
Dim rsBoth
'Build HTML representation of data
    'instantiate concrete builder
Set objBuilder = New HTMLBuilder
objBuilder.FilePath = "d:\DataExport.txt"
    'configure and command director to build
objDirector.Build objBuilder
    'retrieve product form concrete builder
sHTMLParent = objBuilder.GetProduct(partParent)
sHTMLChild = objBuilder.GetProduct(partChild)
sHTMLBoth = objBuilder.GetProduct(partAll)

'Build ADO representation of data
Set objBuilder = New ADOBuilder
objBuilder.FilePath = "d:\DataExport.txt"
objDirector.Build objBuilder
Set rsParent = objBuilder.GetProduct(partParent)
Set rsChild = objBuilder.GetProduct(partChild)
rsBoth = objBuilder.GetProduct(partAll)
End Sub
```

The following code is for the IBuilder class that is an abstract interface. The ProductPart Enum declared in the beginning of the code is used as a parameter of GetProduct to allow a client to specify which part of the product to return.

```
'****************IBuilder*********************
Public Enum ProductPart
    partParent
    partChild
```

```
        partAll
End Enum

Public Sub BuildParents()

End Sub

Public Sub BuildChildren()

End Sub


Public Function GetProduct(Part As ProductPart) As Variant

End Function


Public Property Let FilePath(Path As String)

End Property
```

HTMLBuilder iterates through the rows of data and adds HTML table tags to each column and row. It implements GetProduct by returning the generated HTML as a string.

```
'**************HTMLBuilder********************************
Implements IBuilder
Dim objFSO As New FileSystemObject
Dim sPath As String
Dim sHTMLParent As String
Dim sHTMLChild As String
Private Property Let IBuilder_FilePath(Value As String)
    sPath = Value
End Property

Private Sub IBuilder_BuildChildren()
'creates an html table for each set of child records
Dim sLine As String
Dim vLine As Variant
Dim sLink As String
Dim sHeading As String
Dim sID As String
```

```
Dim sNewID As String
Dim i As Integer
Dim bNewTable As Boolean
Dim objTxt As TextStream
Set objTxt = objFSO.OpenTextFile(sPath, ForReading)
With objTxt
    Do Until .AtEndOfStream              'loop until end of file
        sLine = .ReadLine                'read first line
        If sLine = "&child" Then
            sLine = .ReadLine
            'tag line
            sLine = Replace(sLine, vbTab, "</th><th>")
            'add missing tags
            sLine = "<tr><th>" & sLine & "</th></tr>"
            sHeading = sLine
            Do Until .AtEndOfStream
                sLine = .ReadLine
                'foreign key linking to parent
                sNewID=LeftsLine,InStr(1,sLine,vbTab)-1)
            'if new set of children then create new table
                If sNewID <> sID Then
            'if not first table then need closing table tag
                    If sID > "" Then
                        sHTMLChild = sHTMLChild & _
"</table><p><table>" & sHeading
                    Else
                        sHTMLChild=sHTMLChild & "<table>" _
                        & sHeading
                    End If
            'note that is new table in order to append link to first row
                    bNewTable = True
                    sID = sNewID
                Else
                    bNewTable = False
                End If
                sLine = Replace(sLine, vbTab, "</td><td>")
                sLine = "<tr><td>" & sLine & "</td></tr>"
                If bNewTable = True Then
                    'append link to parent
                    sHTMLChild=sHTMLChild & "<a name=" & _
                    sID & "></a>"
                End If
```

```vb
                sHTMLChild = sHTMLChild & sLine
            DoEvents
            Loop
            sHTMLChild = sHTMLChild & "</table>"
        End If
        DoEvents
    Loop
End With
End Sub

Private Sub IBuilder_BuildParents()
Dim sLine As String
Dim vLine As Variant
Dim sLink As String
Dim sID As String
Dim i As Integer
Dim objTxt As TextStream
Set objTxt = objFSO.OpenTextFile(sPath, ForReading)
With objTxt
    Do Until .AtEndOfStream
        If Trim(sLine) = "&child" Then Exit Do
        sLine = .ReadLine
        If Trim(sLine) = "&parent" Then
            sLine = .ReadLine
            sLine = Replace(sLine, vbTab, "</th><th>")
            sHTMLParent="<table><tr><th>" & sLine & _ "</th></tr>"
            Do Until .AtEndOfStream
                sLine = .ReadLine
                If Trim(sLine) = "&child" Then Exit Do
                sID=Left(sLine, InStr(1, sLine, vbTab) - 1)
                sLine=Replace(sLine, vbTab, "</td><td>", _ InStr(1, _
    sLine, vbTab) + 1)
                sHTMLParent=sHTMLParent & "<tr><td><a" & _ "href=" &_
                "#" & sID & ">" & sID & "</a></td><td>" & _ "sLine & "<_
                td></tr>"
                DoEvents
            Loop
            sHTMLParent = sHTMLParent & "</table>"
        End If
        DoEvents
    Loop
End With
End Sub
```

```
Private Function IBuilder_GetProduct(Part As ProductPart) As Variant
Select Case Part
Case partParent
    IBuilder_GetProduct = sHTMLParent
Case partChild
    IBuilder_GetProduct = sHTMLChild
Case partAll
    IBuilder_GetProduct = sHTMLParent & sHTMLChild
End Select
End Function
```

The following code is for ADOBuilder, which is a concrete class of IBuilder. It builds a disconnected ADO recordset out of the data by appending a field to a recordset for each column of data in the text file, and then populates the recordset with the actual data. It implements GetProduct by returning ADO recordsets.

```
'***************ADOBuilder*********************
Implements IBuilder
Dim objFSO As New FileSystemObject
Dim rsParent As ADODB.Recordset
Dim rsChild As ADODB.Recordset
Dim sPath As String

Private Sub IBuilder_BuildChildren()
    BuildTable partChild
End Sub

Private Sub IBuilder_BuildParents()
    BuildTable partParent
End Sub


Private Property Let IBuilder_FilePath(Value As String)
    sPath = Value
End Property

Private Function IBuilder_GetProduct(Part As ProductPart) As Variant
Dim vRS(1)
Select Case Part
Case partParent
    Set IBuilder_GetProduct = rsParent
Case partChild
```

```
            Set IBuilder_GetProduct = rsChild
Case partAll
        Set vRS(0) = rsParent
        Set vRS(1) = rsChild
        IBuilder_GetProduct = vRS
End Select

End Function

Private Function BuildTable(Part As ProductPart)
Dim sPart As String
Dim sNotPart As String
Dim rs As ADODB.Recordset
Dim sLine As String
Dim vLine As Variant
Dim i As Integer
        Select Case Part
        Case partParent
            sPart = "&parent"
            sNotPart = "&child"
            Set rsParent = New ADODB.Recordset
            Set rs = rsParent
        Case partChild
            sPart = "&child"
            sNotPart = "&parent"
            Set rsChild = New ADODB.Recordset
            Set rs = rsChild
        End Select
        Dim objTxt As TextStream
        Set objTxt = objFSO.OpenTextFile(sPath, ForReading)
        With objTxt
            Do Until .AtEndOfStream
'if building parents and have reached child section then exit
                If Trim(sLine) = sNotPart And Part = partParent Then_
    Exit Do
                sLine = .ReadLine
                'if we have reached desired section
                If Trim(sLine) = sPart Then
                    'read the next line
                    sLine = .ReadLine
                    'turn it into an array
```

```
                        vLine = Split(sLine, vbTab)
                        'build disconected recordset
                        For i = 0 To UBound(vLine)
                                rs.Fields.Append vLine(i), _ adVarChar, 255
                        Next i
                        'open recordset
                        rs.Open
                        Do Until .AtEndOfStream
                                sLine = .ReadLine
            'if we have reached next section then exit
                                If Trim(sLine)=sNotPart Then Exit Do
                                vLine = Split(sLine, vbTab)
                                rs.AddNew
                                For i = 0 To UBound(vLine)
                                        rs.Fields(i) = vLine(i)
                                Next i
                                rs.Update
                                DoEvents
                        Loop
                    End If
                Loop
                On Error Resume Next
                rs.MoveFirst
                On Error GoTo 0
                .Close
            End With
    End Function
```

Related Patterns

The builder pattern is similar to the abstract factory pattern in that they both provide a constant interface for producing complex objects. The difference between
the two is that builder allows for control over the building process by exposing
each step of the process as a public method. Abstract factory, on the other hand,
only takes a command that tells it to build and then returns the final product.
Abstract factory also differentiates itself by specializing in producing a family of
related objects.

> **NOTE** Learn more about the abstract factory pattern in Chapter 23, "The Factory Pattern."

Conclusion

The builder pattern is best suited for when you want to represent complex objects in multiple formats. By separating the builder object's interface from its implementation, the builder pattern allows you to create multiple implementations and still keep things simple for client objects. The builder pattern is good for producing complex objects because it gives you the ability to configure the final product by controlling the building process.

chapter 26

The Prototype Pattern

- Implementing a prototype pattern

- A UML diagram of a prototype pattern

- A sample use of a prototype pattern

- Other uses of a prototype

- Related patterns

The *prototype* pattern provides a method to create objects by cloning pre-existing objects. It allows clients to create new objects, not by instantiating the object, but by asking another object, the prototype, to clone itself. By using the prototype pattern, you can internalize the instantiation and initialization of new objects into the class itself.

Implementing the prototype pattern in Visual Basic can prove to be tedious. This is because Visual Basic does not provide any inherent ability to clone an object. In some languages, like SmallTalk, cloning is built into the base object. If this were the case in Visual Basic, the `Object` class—from which all other objects in VB are subclassed—would have a clone method.

You should use the prototype pattern in any instance where you need to provide a very flexible interface for creating new objects. At run time, a set of objects can be instantiated as prototypes. In addition to just instantiating the objects, you could set the objects to an initial state. This state would then be copied into all of its clones. By allowing the prototypes to build themselves, you remove the client from having to initialize each object. This type of architecture is great for building frameworks that do not know about the type of objects or the state of the objects. Since frameworks are often built prior to any specific implementation, the need for a dynamic method of instantiating objects and setting their initial state is a requirement.

Implementing a Prototype Pattern

There are several issues that arise during the implementation of the prototype pattern in Visual Basic. First, there is no built-in method to clone objects. The Visual Basic base class, Object, does not have a clone method. There is also no API call that can be made to create a copy of an object. So every class that you want to be a prototype must both implement its own version of a clone method and be able to set the properties of the cloned object.

It is very easy to implement a simple clone method:

```
Implements IPrototype
Private Function IPrototype_Clone() As IPrototype
    Set Clone = New clsComponent
End Function
```

Here, the clone method just returns a pointer to a new instance of itself (clsComponent). This would be great if all you needed to do was return a new instance of the class, but the power of the prototype pattern is that you can set the state of the prototype and then all of the clones would inherit this default state. By doing this you could have one class that is used in many different contexts. This state is added during the initialization of the new instance.

Initializing the state of a cloned object is problematic in Visual Basic. The prototype pattern provides its flexibility by allowing you to create a pool of objects that have been initialized to some state. You can then clone these objects and be assured that the state of the clone is the same as its prototype.

A graphics application is a good way to illustrate the prototype pattern. In the graphics application you can have a generic class called clsGraphic. This class could be initialized in several different states, like line, rectangle, and circle. In code we could have the following behind a form:

```
Private oRectangleGraphic As clsGraphic
Private oLineGraphic As clsGraphic
Private oCircleGraphic As clsGraphic

Private Sub NewRectangle(x As Long, y As Long, Width As Long, _
    Height As Long)
    Dim oNewRectangle As clsGraphic

    Set oNewRectangle = oRectangleGraphic.Clone
    oNewRectangle.Draw x, y, Width, Height
End Sub

Private Sub Form_Load()
    Set oRectangleGraphic = New clsGraphic
    oRectangleGraphic.BitmapFile = "c:\rectangle.bmp"

    Set oLineGraphic = New clsGraphic
    oLineGraphic.BitmapFile = "c:\Line.bmp"

    Set oCircleGraphic = New clsGraphic
    oCircleGraphic.BitmapFile = "c:\circle.bmp"
End Sub
```

This simple example just creates a pool of graphic prototypes in the Form_Load event and then draws a rectangle based on the oRectangleGraphic prototype. By coding the application in this manner, the clsGraphic class does not need to know anything about rectangles and circles.

In this example, the initialization of each clone is simple because the clsGraphic class exposes the properties as public properties, so the Clone method is simply:

```
Private sBitmapPath As String

Public Property Get Clone() As clsGraphic
    Set Clone = New clsGraphic
    Clone.BitmapFile = sBitmapPath
End Property
```

The clone method creates an instance and then sets the BitmapFile to the same file path that the prototype was initialized with. The real problem of initializing a clone object arises when you need to copy public and private state as well as cloning object references stored in the prototype.

One method to set the initial state of public and private properties in a class is to add an Init method to the class like the following:

```
Private sName As String
Private lID As Long

Public Property Get Name() As String
    Name = sName
End Property
Public Sub Init(Name As String, ID As Long)
    sName = Name
    lID = ID
End Sub
```

Here, the parameters of the Init method represent the public and private variables of the class. You can take this further by passing in any collection of parameters into the Init method using structures like an array, XML, or a Parameters collection you create.

The last issue has to do with cloning object references that are within the Prototype object. You could simply create a clone that points to the same objects in the prototype. This type of cloning is called shallow cloning. Shallow cloning allows a prototype and the cloned object to share child objects. New instances of the children are not created, but a pointer to the same child is contained in each object.

The other method is if you also clone the object reference in the prototype. This method of cloning is called deep cloning. Deep cloning provides independence between the clone and the prototype, but it forces you to clone each object within the prototype. An example of shallow cloning would be:

```
Private oCollection As Collection

Public Sub Clone() As clsGenericClass
     Set Clone = New clsGenericClass
     Clone.Init oCollection
End Sub

Public Sub Init(pCollection As Collection)
     Set oCollection = pCollection
End Sub
```

An example of deep cloning would be:

```
Private oRS As ADODB.Recordset

Public Sub Clone() As clsGenericClass
     Set Clone = New clsGenericClass
     Clone.Init oRS.Clone
End Sub

Public Sub Init(Recordset As ADODB.Recordset)
     Set oRS = Recordset
End Sub
```

This example takes advantage of the Clone method of the Recordset object in ADO to provide deep cloning. If you are implementing deep cloning on custom classes, you will also need to implement the clone method on each of the classes.

A UML Diagram of a Prototype Pattern

Figure 26.1 depicts a class diagram of the prototype pattern.

FIGURE 26.1
A class diagram of the
prototype pattern

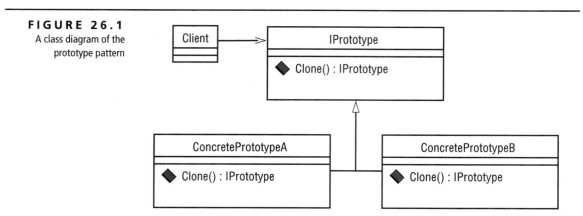

The prototype pattern consists of an IPrototype interface and ConcretePrototypes. The IPrototype interface defines the Clone method. The ConcretePrototype classes implement the IPrototype interface. They implement the specific functionality for cloning themselves. The Clone method returns a copy of itself.

A Sample Use of a Prototype Pattern

At some point, every developer has been asked to create a form that allows the user to copy the information they have already entered before the user begins entering new information. Users want an easy way to copy the data of an existing entry in order to produce a second instance. This type of cloning can be handled by implementing the prototype pattern in your application. Figure 26.2 shows an example of an order entry application that uses the prototype pattern.

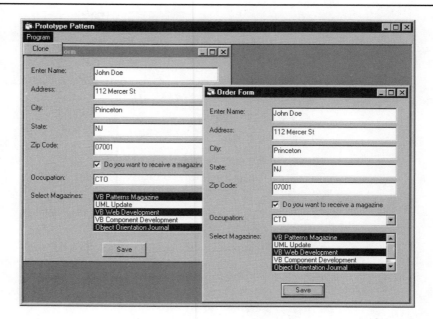

This application will allow the user to enter information in one form and then select the clone menu option to clone the form and all of its information. The user can then make a few adjustments and save the new form without having to enter all of the information again.

Figure 26.3 depicts the class diagram for the order entry application.

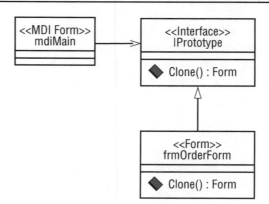

The application is made of two forms and one abstract interface. The IPrototype interface defines only one method, the Clone method. The interface is defined as follows:

```
' IPrototype - Abstract Interface

Option Explicit

Public Function Clone() As Form
End Function
```

The frmOrderForm implements the IPrototype interface. It is the Concrete-Prototype object in the application. The implementation of the Clone method is as follows:

```
' frmOrderForm code module

Option Explicit

Implements IPrototype

Private Function IPrototype_Clone() As Form
    Dim oClone As frmOrderForm

    Set oClone = New frmOrderForm

    Init oClone

    Set IPrototype_Clone = oClone
End Function
```

This method creates a new instance of the frmOrderForm form and calls the Init method to initialize the form. The Init method sets the initial state of the cloned form. It populates the controls of the cloned form with the data in the prototype. The code for the Init method is shown below:

```
Private Sub Init(Clone As frmOrderForm)
    Dim oControl As Control
    Dim i As Integer

    For Each oControl In Me.Controls
        Select Case TypeName(oControl)
            Case "TextBox"
                Clone.Controls(oControl.Name).Text = oControl.Text
```

```
            Case "CommandButton"
                Clone.Controls(oControl.Name).Caption = _
                oControl.Caption
            Case "Label"
                Clone.Controls(oControl.Name).Caption = _
                oControl.Caption
            Case "ListBox"
                For i = 0 To oControl.ListCount - 1
                    Clone.Controls(oControl.Name).Selected(i) = _
                    oControl.Selected(i)
                Next
            Case "ComboBox"
                Clone.Controls(oControl.Name).ListIndex = _
                oControl.ListIndex
            Case "CheckBox"
                Clone.Controls(oControl.Name).Value = oControl.Value
        End Select
    Next

    Clone.Height = Me.Height
    Clone.Width = Me.Width
End Sub
```

The code is generic enough to allow for changes in the form. It loops through each control in the form and copies the data over to the cloned form using the Controls collection of the form.

The mdiMain form acts as the client in this application. It handles the creation of the original form and asks the prototype to clone itself when the user presses the Clone menu option. The code behind the form is rather simple and shown below:

```
' mdiMain code module

Option Explicit
Private oOrderForm As frmOrderForm

Private Sub MDIForm_Load()
    Set oOrderForm = New frmOrderForm
    oOrderForm.Show
End Sub
```

```
Private Sub mnuClone_Click()
    Dim oClone As frmOrderForm
    Dim oPrototype As IPrototype

    Set oPrototype = oOrderForm

    Set oClone = oPrototype.Clone
    oClone.Show
End Sub
```

The code for the clone menu option casts the oOrderForm object onto the IPrototype interface and then asks the form to clone itself. It then calls the Show method of the form to display the cloned form.

Other Uses of a Prototype

It is useful to implement the prototype pattern when you have to create instances of an object but, during development, you do not know what the initial state of the object will be. In the sample application discussed here, during the development phase the developer would have no idea what state the form was in, and therefore would not be able create new instances of it easily. The prototype pattern allows you to create new instances based on a prototype object existing in memory. This prototype object handles the creation of the new cloned object and sets the initial state of the clone to mimic its own state.

Related Patterns

The prototype is very similar to the factory pattern, but instead of allowing the factory object to instantiate objects, the prototype pattern allows each class to instantiate itself. The prototype pattern decentralizes the creation process from the factory object to each of the objects that are created. By decentralizing this logic, the prototype patterns allows each prototype to set the state of the new instances.

NOTE   You can learn more about the factory pattern in Chapter 23.

Conclusion

The prototype pattern is useful for when you need to develop applications that instantiate new objects in a state mimicking a prototype object. It allows you to create flexible classes where the state of the object is determined by a prototypical object. Client applications can create a pool of prototype objects that have their state set at the beginning of the application; and then any time a new instance of the prototype is required, the client application can ask the prototype to clone itself.

Recommended Books

This appendix contains a list of books on Programming Design Patterns, Architectural Design Patterns, and UML.

Programming Design Patterns

Brown, William J., Raphael C. Malveau, Hays W. McCormick III, William H. Brown, and Thomas J. Mowbray. *AntiPatterns: Refactoring Software, Architectures, and Projects in Crisis*, John Wiley & Sons (1998), ISBN 0-471-19713-0.

Buschman, F, et al. *Pattern Oriented Software Architecture: A System of Patterns*, John Wiley & Sons (1996), ISBN 0-471-95869-7.

Coad, P., D. North, and M. Mayfield. *Object Models: Strategies, Patterns, and Applications*, Yourdon (1996), ISBN 0-13-840117-9

Coplien, J. *Advanced C++ Programming Styles and Idioms*, Addison-Wesley (1991), ISBN 0-201-54855-0.

Coplien, J., and D. Schmidt. *Pattern Languages of Program Design*, Addison-Wesley (1995), ISBN 0-201-60734-4.

Fowler, Martin. *Analysis Patterns: Reusable Object Models*, Addison-Wesley (1996), ISBN 0-201-89542-0.

Gamma, E., R. Helm, R. Johnson, and J. Vlissides. *Design Patterns, Elements of Reusable Object-Oriented Software*, Addison-Wesley (1994), ISBN 0-201-63361-2.

Grand, Mark. *Patterns in Java, Volume 1: A Catalog of Reusable Design Patterns Illustrated with UML*, John Wiley & Sons (1998), ISBN 0-471-25839-3.

Hay, David. *Data Model Patterns: Conventions of Thought*, Dorset House (1995), ISBN 0-932633-29-3.

Martin, R, et al. *Pattern Languages of Program Design 3*, Addison-Wesley (1997), ISBN 0-201-31011-2.

Mowbray, Thomas and Raphael C. Malveau. *Corba Design Patterns*, John Wiley & Sons (1997), ISBN 0-471-15882-8.

Pree, Wolfgang. *Design Patterns for Object-Oriented Development*, Addison-Wesley. (1995), ISBN 0-201-42294-8.

Vlissides, John, J. Coplien, and Norman Kerth. *Pattern Languages of Program Design 2*, Addison-Wesley (1996), ISBN 0-201-89527-7.

Vlissides, John. *Pattern Hatching: Design Patterns Applied*, Addison-Wesley (1998), ISBN 0-201-43293-5.

Architectural Design Patterns

Alexander, Christopher, Sara Ishikawa, and Murray Silverstein. *A Pattern Language: Towns, Buildings, Construction*, Oxford University Press (1977), ISBN 0-19-501919-9.

Unified Modeling Language

Boggs, Wendy, and Michael Boggs. *Mastering UML with Rational Rose*, Sybex, Inc. (1999), ISBN 0-7821-2453-4.

Booch, Grady, Ivar Jacobson and James Rumbaugh. *The Unified Modeling Language User Guide*, Addison-Wesley (1998), ISBN 0-201-57168-4.

Booch, Grady, Ivar Jacobson, and James Rumbaugh. *The Unified Modeling Language Reference Manual*, Addison-Wesley (1999), ISBN 0-201-30998-X.

Fowler, Martin and Kendall Scott. *UML Distilled: Applying the Standard Object Modeling Language*, Addison-Wesley (1996), ISBN 0-201-32563-2.

Oestereich, Bernd. *Developing Software with UML*, Addison-Wesley (1999), ISBN 0-201-39826-5.

Page-Jones, Meilir, *Fundamentals of Object-Oriented Design in UML*, Addison-Wesley (1999), ISBN 0-201-6994-6.

Texel, P., and C. Williams, *Use Cases Combined with Booch, OMT, UML: Processes and Products*, Prentice Hall (1997), ISBN 0-13-727405-X.

Recommended Web Sites

This appendix lists some helpful resources on the Internet that will assist you in your journey through patterns. The appendix lists several different types of resources including:

- Web Sites devoted to patterns
- Articles about patterns
- Frequently Asked Questions
- Mailing Lists

This is by no means an exhaustive list of resources. Rather, it is meant as a starting place for users. A more complete listing of links will be provided on this book's accompanying Web site (which you can access through `www.sybex.com` or `www.flashcreative.com`). In addition, most of the sites and articles listed here provide more links.

Web Sites Devoted to Patterns

The following Web sites will provide you with extensive information about using design patterns in code development.

`http://hillside.net/patterns/` The home page for patterns on the World Wide Web can be found at hillside.net. This site offers many links to other Web sites, conferences, articles, and mailing lists. It is a great place to begin your online search of patterns.

`http://c2.com/ppr/index.html` The Portland Pattern Repository is another great Web site to learn about patterns. It is run by Ward Cunningham and contains the original Wiki Web. The Wiki is the largest on the Web and contains an incredible wealth of knowledge.

`http://wiki.cs.uiuc.edu/PatternStories` The University of Illinois at Urbana-Champaign has started a Wiki on using patterns. This is the place were people have posted their experiences with using patterns in development projects. It is a great place to get ideas on how people are using the patterns described in this book. Most of the stories are about implementations in Java and C++, but you can apply many of the discussions to your VB projects.

`http://www.patterndepot.com/pages/`   The Pattern Depot is a new Web site that was started as a catalog of patterns on the Web. It currently does not have too many patterns in its catalog, but there are a few interesting ones there.

Articles about Patterns

There are thousands of articles about patterns on the Web. There are too many to catalog in this appendix and the list is constantly changing. However, the following links will point you to some interesting articles.

`http://www.enteract.com/~bradapp/docs/patterns-intro.html`   This web page provides is a great place to start when reading about patterns. The page covers the gamut of topics related to patterns, from defining pattern-to-pattern languages to writing your own patterns.

`http://hillside.net/patterns/definition.html`   Written by James Coplien, this article provides a good definition of what a pattern is.

`http://g.oswego.edu/dl/ca/ca/ca.html`   A good introduction to patterns based on the writings of the originator of patterns, Christopher Alexander. It defines what a pattern is from Alexander's perspective and then goes into details about the properties of patterns.

`http://www.agcs.com/patterns/papers/patterns.htm`   An introduction to patterns that also provides a template for writing patterns.

`http://c2.com/doc/oopsla87.html`   Outlines a pattern language for developing object orientated programs.

`http://www.agcs.com/patterns/papers/index.htm`   Many great articles on patterns written by members of AG Communication Systems.

`ftp://members.aol.com/kgb1001001/Chasms/chasms.pdf`   An interesting article from Kyle Brown on creating a pattern language for interactions between object-oriented systems and relational databases.

`http://www.stevenblack.com/SBC%20Publications.asp`   Steven Black has written several good articles on design patterns and Visual FoxPro.

`http://hometown.aol.com/kgb1001001/Articles/threetier/`
`threetier.htm`   This article creates a pattern language for developing three-tier distributed application. It presents patterns in three areas, architectural patterns, organizational patterns, and implementation patterns.

`http://www1.bell-labs.com/user/cope/Patterns/Process/RAPPeL/`
`rapel.html`   This page presents RAPPeL, A Requirements Analysis Process Pattern Language for Object-Oriented Development. It provides patterns for defining and determining requirements for business applications.

`http://www1.bell-labs.com/user/cope/Patterns/`
`IeeeSoftwareSpecialPatternIssue.html`   James Coplien presents a history of patterns and the relations of patterns to software architecture and object-oriented systems.

`http://www.pliant.org/personal/Tom_Erickson/`
`DesignLinguaFranca.html`   Thomas Erickson describes a pattern language for user interface design in this article in order to create a common language for user interface specialists.

`http://www-dse.doc.ic.ac.uk/~np2/patterns/scripting/index.html`
This article presents a pattern language for developing for scripting languages. This is a helpful article for developers working in VBScript.

`http://www.agcs.com/patterns/papers/tutnotes/index.htm`   This page introduces developers to patterns through the use of non-software examples.

FAQ

The frequently asked questions page for patterns is maintained at `http://g.oswego.edu/dl/pd-FAQ/pd-FAQ.html`. It provides some quick answers to common questions that have been asked in the pattern-discussion list.

Mailing Lists

The University of Illinois at Urban-Champaign maintains several mailing lists that provide a wealth of information on patterns.

- patterns@cs.uiuc.edu is for presenting and describing software patterns.

- business-patterns@cs.uiuc.edu is for presenting and describing business patterns.

- patterns-discussion@cs.uiuc.edu is for discussion of patterns in general.

- gang-of-4-patterns@cs.uiuc.edu is about the design patterns in the Gang of Four's book.

- siemens-patterns@cs.uiuc.edu is about the patterns described by the Siemens guys.

- organization-patterns@cs.uiuc.edu is for discussing patterns involving organizations.

- antipatterns@cs.uiuc.edu concerns antipattern refactoring and the book AntiPatterns.

- telecom-patterns@cs.uiuc.edu is about patterns for telecommunications.

You can subscribe to any of these mailing lists at http://st-www.cs.uiuc.edu/users/brant/subscribe.html.

The archive for each of these mailing lists is maintained by DistributedObjects.com and can be found at http://www.distributedobjects.com/portfolio/archives/patterns/index.html.

List of Patterns

This appendix lists all of the patterns from this book in alphabetical order, including the pattern type and a short description. Here, you can quickly zero in on the pattern you are searching for. You will also find the chapter number so you can quickly read more details about the selected pattern.

Pattern Name	Pattern Type	Pattern Description	Chapter Number
Adapter	Structural	The adapter pattern, otherwise known as a wrapper pattern, allows two objects to communicate even though they have incompatible interfaces. The adapter pattern accomplishes this by using an intermediary object that is compliant with the client object and delegates the execution of the client requests to the incompatible server object.	5
Bridge	Structural	A bridge pattern allows you to separate an interface from its implementation, so that the two can vary independently. You use a bridge pattern when you want to vary the implementation of a particular method at runtime, and you don't want to recompile the client code. This pattern also allows you to standardize an implementation across multiple classes by bridging all the interface classes to one implementation object.	4
Builder	Creational	The builder pattern provides a mechanism for building objects that separates the interface which builds the object from its implementation so that the same interface can be used to build different types of objects. This allows you to modify the implementation of a builder without breaking existing clients, and to easily add implementations that will be compatible with existing clients.	25

Pattern Name	Pattern Type	Pattern Description	Chapter Number
Chain of Responsibility	Behavioral	The chain of responsibility pattern is an extremely flexible and extensible pattern. This pattern decouples the sender of a request from its receiver by giving more than one object a chance to handle the request. The request is passed along a group or "chain" of objects. The chain of responsibility pattern is used when more than one object can handle a request, but the requesting object does not know which object should answer the request.	13
Command	Behavioral	The command pattern is used to turn a client procedure call into an object. This pattern gives the procedure request a life of its own so that it can have its own behaviors and properties. The command object does not carry out the request; rather it receives the request from the client, performs the functionality that it was designed to do, and then passes the request to the server object that is able to carry out the client's request. The command pattern allows you to add intelligence and behavior to procedure calls without modifying the client or server.	14
Composite	Structural	The composite pattern provides a unified interface that both collection classes and leaf node classes can inherit. By defining one interface, clients can treat items and collections uniformly within a hierarchy. Client code can recursively iterate through a part-whole hierarchy without having to write separate code to distinguish between the collections and primitives. The composite pattern eliminates the need to write case statements that depend on the type of class when traversing a hierarchy.	6

Pattern Name	Pattern Type	Pattern Description	Chapter Number
Decorator	Structural	The decorator pattern allows additional responsibilities to be assigned to an object without subclassing It allows an object to add new functionality to another object dynamically. The decorator pattern can be used as an alternative to implementation inheritance. The decorator pattern encloses an object within a decorator object that adds additional functionality without modifying the interface of the original object. Since the interface is not modified and must be implemented completely by the decorator object, multiple decorators can be stacked in order to provide layers of functionality that are added dynamically to a component.	7
Facade	Structural	The facade pattern provides a relatively simple interface to a complex subsystem or set of subsystems. This pattern is used when a system provides its services through multiple subsystems or through calling multiple procedures. In order for clients to use the services of the system they would have to be familiar with the intricacies of its subsystems and procedures. The facade pattern shields clients from the intricacies of the subsystems by providing a simple interface for clients to call. The facade in turn makes the necessary calls to its constituents to provide the service.	8

Pattern Name	Pattern Type	Pattern Description	Chapter Number
Factory	Creational	The factory pattern provides a mechanism to separate a client from the process of creating a set of related objects or products. It provides an interface to delegate the creation of objects without specifying the concrete class. The factory encapsulates the rules for instantiating objects and buffers the client from the knowledge of the concrete class that is being instantiated.	23
Flyweight	Structural	The flyweight pattern provides a method to pool and share a large number of contexts. It allows a single object to be used in several contexts simultaneously. It is a pattern that allows applications to be designed from an object-oriented view without the cost of instantiating a large amount of objects, which could be prohibitive and inefficient.	9
Hook	Behavioral	The hook pattern allows developers to build flexibility into their code. By letting them (or later developers) implement currently undefined functionality for the future. A hook is simply a call from within a working procedure to an unimplemented procedure, meaning a procedure that consists of only the procedure stub without any implementation code. The call to the procedure is known as the hook, and the empty procedure is known as the hook operation. The hook operation is where code for future functionality will be written.	19

Pattern Name	Pattern Type	Pattern Description	Chapter Number
Interpreter	Behavioral	Interpreter is used to help an application understand a natural language statement and execute the intended functionality of that statement. Interpreter-type functionality is used every day by developers in the form of code compilers and utilities that execute SQL statements. There are many algorithms that can be used to provide this functionality; some algorithms provide good performance whereas others minimize resource consumption. The benefit of the interpreter pattern is the flexibility that it provides; it allows you to easily add new syntax rules and multiple implementations of a statement.	15
Iterator	Behavioral	The iterator pattern provides a method to sequentially access members of a collection. This pattern separates the traversal mechanism and state management from an aggregate object. It removes the interface to traverse a group of objects from the aggregate object without revealing the underlying representation. Removing the mechanism to iterate through the collection allows different algorithms, such as a forward iteration and a reverse iteration, to be used to step through the collection without bloating the collection interface. In addition, the iterator pattern allows multiple clients to iterate through the same collection and be at different points.	16

Pattern Name	Pattern Type	Pattern Description	Chapter Number
Mediator	Behavioral	The mediator pattern creates an object (the mediator) that acts like a traffic cop, controlling the interaction between a set of objects. The mediator encapsulates the rules of interaction between the set of objects by loosely coupling the objects: the objects are not aware of each other, they are only aware of the mediator object. All "traffic" goes through the mediator.	12
Memento	Behavioral	The memento pattern is used when an object needs to record its current state so that it can be restored to that state at a later time. The memento pattern is best suited for externalizing the state of an object when you can't or don't want to burden the originator with implementing the storing and restoration of state. In cases where you have to externalize protected data, the design of memento allows you to hide that data from the objects that handle it.	20
Observer	Behavioral	The observer pattern defines a one-to-many dependency between objects so that when one object changes state, all of its dependents are notified and updated automatically. There are two main types of observers: *pull observers* and *push observers*, which differ in how the observer relates to its subject or subjects.	11

Pattern Name	Pattern Type	Pattern Description	Chapter Number
Prototype	Creational	The prototype pattern provides a method to create objects by cloning pre-exisising objects. It allows clients to create new objects, not by instantiating the object, but by asking another object—the prototype—to clone itself. By using the prototype pattern, you can internalize the instantiation and initialization of new objects into the class itself.	26
Proxy	Structural	The proxy pattern provides a surrogate object that delegates method calls to another object. It acts like a placeholder for an object that can be used to efficiently control access to the other object. The proxy mimics the other object to the extent that the client does not know that it is communicating with a proxy. The proxy pattern is used whenever you need an object to receive method calls on behalf of another object.	10
Singleton	Creational	The singleton pattern ensures that only one instance of a class exists at any time. It forces client applications to work with only one instance of a class and will not allow them to instantiate more then one instance. It provides a single, global point of access for clients to work with a resource.	24

Pattern Name	Pattern Type	Pattern Description	Chapter Number
State	Behavioral	The state pattern allows an object's implementation to change at runtime depending on the internal state of the object. It provides a way to alter the behavior of an object whenever the state of the object changes. To achieve this, the object delegates its behavior to encapsulated state specific objects.	21
Strategy	Behavioral	The strategy pattern abstracts a family of algorithms into individual objects that share a common interface so that they can be used interchangeably. A family of algorithms is a group of calculations that aim to solve the same problem in different ways. The strategy pattern calls for the separate algorithms to be encapsulated in individual objects that conform to common interface. The client is bound to the interface, and can be dynamically pointed to use any one of the individual strategy objects.	22

Pattern Name	Pattern Type	Pattern Description	Chapter Number
Template Method	Behavioral	The template method pattern is a simple, yet fundamental pattern for code reuse. The key to this pattern is putting the skeleton of an algorithm within a method (the Template Method). Steps in the algorithm become methods called from the template method. This keeps the overall algorithm constant, while allowing you to change how the individual steps of the algorithm are carried out. The template method is best suited for when you are implementing a defined algorithm. It helps you avoid spaghetti code by standardizing the steps of the code first and then implementing each individual step.	18
Visitor	Behavioral	The visitor pattern is used when operations must be performed upon numerous elements of an object model. Without the visitor, this type of functionality is usually implemented by spreading the required operations throughout the object model. Visitor provides a clean and more flexible model by abstracting the operations from the elements of the object model and turning them into visitor objects. The visitor objects traverse the object model and perform their respective operations upon the individual elements. The visitor pattern allows you to keep an object model neat by abstracting the operations that have to be performed on the elements of the model into separate objects. It also allows you to easily add or remove operations without touching the elements of the model.	17

INDEX

Note to the Reader: Page numbers in **bold** indicate the principle discussion of a topic or the definition of a term. Page numbers in *italic* indicate illustrations.

D

defined, **14–15**
sequence diagrams, 14–15
state diagrams, 15
design time reuse, **26**
Developing Software with UML (Oestereich), 287
Director class, **263**, 264
DLLs, ActiveX, singleton pattern in, 253–254
DLLs, non-COM, VBScript calling, *50*, 50–51
document editors, flyweight pattern and, 95–96
dynamic object substitution, **34–37**

E

Erickson, Thomas, 292
event hooks, 203, 208
Execute method, *133*, 133–135, 136, 138
EXEs, ActiveX, singleton pattern in, **254**
EXEs, Standard, singleton pattern in, 250–252
external iterators, **167**
extrinsic state of objects, **94–95**, 96

F

facade pattern, **88–92**, *See also* structural patterns
adapter pattern and, 57
command pattern and, 147
decorator pattern and, 91–92
defined, **88, 298**
mediator pattern and, 92, 128
overview of, 92

patterns related to, 91–92
proxy pattern and, 108
sample use of, 89–91, *90*
UML diagram of, 88, *89*
factory methods, 189, 193, 248
factory pattern, **240–248**, *See also* creational patterns
abstract factories, 47, 240–242, *242*, 270
bridge pattern and, 47
builder pattern and, 270
concrete factories, 241, *243*, 243
defined, **240, 299**
factory method pattern and, 248
flyweight pattern and, 100
hook methods in, 243–244, *244*
hook pattern and, 208
implementing, 240–241
other uses of, 247
overview of, 248
parameterized factories, 241, *243*, 243
patterns related to, 248
prototype pattern and, 282
purpose of, 47
sample use of, 244–247, *245–246*
singleton pattern and, 248, 257
template method pattern and, 198
family of algorithms, **230**
FAQs Web page, 292
filter iterators, *170*, 170, 173–174
flyweight pattern, **94–100**, *See also* structural patterns
composite pattern and, 72, 100
defined, **94, 299**
document editors and, 95–96
factory pattern and, 100
flyweight objects, 94, *96*, 96

V

virtual proxy, **102–103**, 107
visitor pattern, **178–186**, *See also* behavioral
  patterns
  composite pattern and, 186
  defined, **178**, **304**
  implementing, 178–179
  interpreter pattern and, 151, 162
  iterator pattern and, 186
  overview of, 186
  patterns related to, 186
  sample code for, 183–185
  sample use of, 181–183, *182–183*
  UML diagram of, *180–181*, 180–181
  uses of, 178, 186
Visual Basic
  cloning objects and, 274–275
  creating design patterns in
    abstract interfaces and, 35–37
    concrete classes and, 35
    dynamic object substitution and, 34–37
    implementations and, 33–34
    implementing decoupled objects, 35–37
    Implements keyword and, 35–37
    inheritance and, 22, 26, 32
    interface objects and, 34–37
    loosely coupled objects and, 33–34
    overview of, 26–27, 37
    public interfaces and, 34
    roles and, 33–34
    sample code, 36–37
    tightly coupled objects and, 33–34
  singleton pattern and, 250, 257
  VBScript calling non-COM DLLs, *50*, 50–51
Vlissides, John, 25, 286, 287
voyeurs. *See* pull observers

W

Web sites
  for design patterns, 290–293
  flashcreative.com, 27, 290
  Sybex, 290
Wiki Web, 290
Wiley, John, 286
Williams, C., 287
Wirfs-Brock, Rebecca, 6
wrapper pattern. *See* adapter pattern

Y

Yourdon, Ed, 6

SYBEX BOOKS ON THE WEB

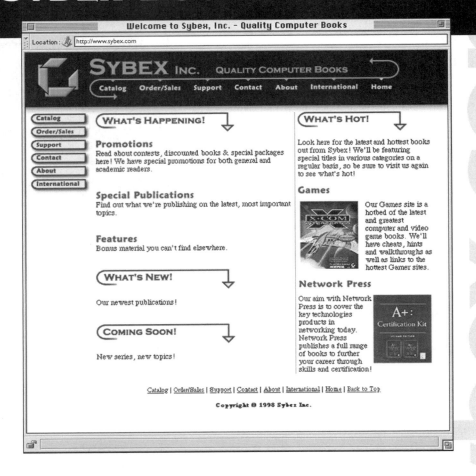

Welcome to Sybex, Inc. - Quality Computer Books

Location: http://www.sybex.com

SYBEX INC. QUALITY COMPUTER BOOKS

Catalog   Order/Sales   Support   Contact   About   International   Home

- Catalog
- Order/Sales
- Support
- Contact
- About
- International

WHAT'S HAPPENING!

Promotions
Read about contests, discounted books & special packages here! We have special promotions for both general and academic readers.

Special Publications
Find out what we're publishing on the latest, most important topics.

Features
Bonus material you can't find elsewhere.

WHAT'S NEW!

Our newest publications!

COMING SOON!

New series, new topics!

WHAT'S HOT!

Look here for the latest and hottest books out from Sybex! We'll be featuring special titles in various categories on a regular basis, so be sure to visit us again to see what's hot!

Games

Our Games site is a hotbed of the latest and greatest computer and video game books. We'll have cheats, hints and walkthroughs as well as links to the hottest Gamer sites.

Network Press

Our aim with Network Press is to cover the key technologies products in networking today. Network Press publishes a full range of books to further your career through skills and certification!

A+: Certification Kit

Catalog | Order/Sales | Support | Contact | About | International | Home | Back to Top.

Copyright © 1998 Sybex Inc.

At the dynamic and informative Sybex Web site, you can:

- view our complete online catalog
- preview a book you're interested in
- access special book content

- order books online at special discount prices
- learn about Sybex

www.sybex.com

SYBEX Inc. • 1151 Marina Village Parkway, Alameda, CA 94501 • 510-523-8233

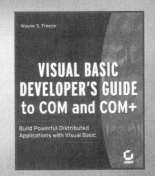